THE COMPUTER & THE BRAI

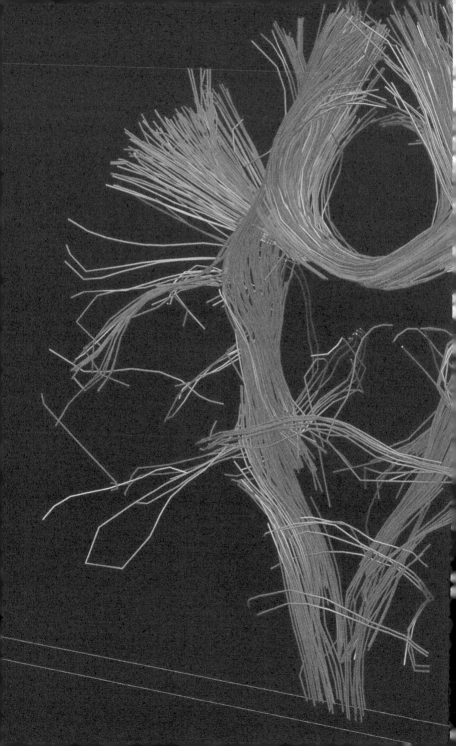

JOHN VON NEUMANN

THE COMPUTER & THE BRAIN

FOREWORD BY RAY KURZWEIL

THIRD EDITION

Yale
UNIVERSITY
PRESS
NEW HAVEN
& LONDON

First edition 1958.
Second edition published as a Yale Nota Bene book in 2000.
Third edition 2012.

Yale University Press books may be purchased in quantity for educational, business, or promotional use. For information, please e-mail sales.press@yale .edu (U.S. office) or sales@yaleup.co.uk (U.K. office).

Library of Congress Control Number: 2011943281
ISBN 978-0-300-18111-1 (pbk.)
A catalogue record for this book is available from the British Library.

Frontispiece: Adapted from "White Matter Tracks Image #20 from the HCP." Courtesy of Arthur W. Toga and Vaughan Greer at the Laboratory of Neuro Imaging at UCLA; Randy Buckner, Bruce Rosen, and Van J. Wedeen at the Martinos Center for Biomedical Imaging at MGH; Consortium of the Human Connectome Project.

10 9 8 7 6 5 4 3 2 1

MIX
Paper from responsible sources
FSC   FSC® C013604
www.fsc.org

Printed and bound by CPI Group (UK) Ltd, Croydon, CR0 4YY

On the foundation established in memory of Mrs. Hepsa Ely Silliman, the President and Fellows of Yale University present an annual course of lectures designed to illustrate the presence and providence of God as manifested in the natural and moral world. It was the belief of the testator that any orderly presentation of the facts of nature or history contributed to this end more effectively than dogmatic or polemical theology, which should therefore be excluded from the scope of the lectures. The subjects are selected rather from the domains of natural science and history, giving special prominence to astronomy, chemistry, geology, and anatomy.

CONTENTS

FOREWORD TO THE THIRD EDITION

Information technologies have already transformed every
facet of human life from business and politics to the arts.
Given the inherent exponential increase in the price-
performance and capacity of every form of information
technology, the information age is continually expanding
its sphere of influence. Arguably the most important information process to understand is human intelligence itself,
and this book is perhaps the earliest serious examination of
the relationship between our thinking and the computer,
from the mathematician who formulated the fundamental
architecture of the computer era.

In a grand project to understand the human brain, we are
making accelerating gains in reverse engineering the paradigms of human thinking, and are applying these biologically inspired methods to create increasingly intelligent
machines. Artificial intelligence (AI) devised in this way will
ultimately soar past unenhanced human thinking. My view
is that the purpose of this endeavor is not to displace us but to

expand the reach of what is already a human-machine civilization. This is what makes our species unique.

So what are the key ideas that underlie this information age? By my count there are five. John von Neumann is largely responsible for three of them, and he made a fundamental contribution to a fourth. Claude Shannon solved the fundamental problem of making information reliable. Alan Turing demonstrated and defined the universality of computation and was influenced by an early lecture by von Neumann. Building on Turing and Shannon, von Neumann created the von Neumann machine, which became—and remains—the fundamental architecture for computation.

In the deceptively modest volume you are now holding, von Neumann articulates his model of computation and goes on to define the essential equivalence of the human brain and a computer. He acknowledges the apparently deep structural differences, but by applying Turing's principle of the equivalence of all computation, von Neumann envisions a strategy to understand the brain's methods as computation, to re-create those methods, and ultimately to expand its powers. The book is all the more prescient given that it was written more than half a century ago when neuroscience had only the most primitive tools available. Finally, von Neumann anticipates the essential acceleration of technology and its inevitable consequences in a coming singular transformation of human existence. Let's consider these five basic ideas in slightly more detail.

Around 1940, if you used the word "computer," people assumed you were talking about an analog computer. Numbers were represented by different levels of voltage, and specialized components could perform arithmetic functions such as addition and multiplication. A big limitation, however, was that analog computers were plagued by accuracy issues. Numbers could be represented with an accuracy of only about one part in a hundred, and because voltage levels representing numbers were processed by increasing numbers of arithmetic operators, these errors would accumulate. If you wanted to perform more than a handful of computations, the results would become so inaccurate as to be meaningless.

Anyone who can remember the days of copying music using analog tape will remember this effect. There was noticeable degradation on the first copy, for it was a little noisier than the original ("noise" represents random inaccuracies). A copy of the copy was noisier still, and by the tenth generation, the copy was almost entirely noise.

It was assumed that the same problem would plague the emerging world of digital computers. We can see this perceived problem if we consider the communication of digital information through a channel. No channel is perfect and will have some inherent error rate. Suppose we have a channel that has a 0.9 probability of correctly transmitting each bit of information. If I send a message that is one-bit long, the probability of accurately transmitting it through that channel will be 0.9. Suppose I send two bits? Now the accuracy is $0.9^2 = 0.81$. How about if I send one byte (eight bits)? I have less than an even chance (0.43, to be exact) of sending it correctly. The probability of accurately sending five bytes is about 1 percent.

An obvious approach to circumvent this problem is to make the channel more accurate. Suppose the channel makes only one error in a million bits. If I send a file with a half million bytes (about the size of a modest program or database), the probability of correctly transmitting it is less than 2 percent, despite the very high inherent accuracy of the channel. Given that a single-bit error can completely invalidate a computer program and other forms of digital data, that is not a satisfactory situation. Regardless of the accuracy of the channel, since the likelihood of an error in a transmission grows rapidly with the size of the message, this would seem to be an intractable problem.

Analog computers approach this problem through graceful degradation. They also accumulate inaccuracies with increased use, but if we limit ourselves to a constrained set of calculations, they prove somewhat useful. Digital computers, on the other hand, require continual communication, not just from one computer to another, but within the computer itself. There is communication between its memory and the central processing unit. Within the central processing unit, there is communication from one register to another, and back and forth to the arithmetic unit, and so on. Even within the arithmetic unit, there is communication from one bit register to another. Communication is pervasive at every level. If we consider that error rates escalate rapidly with increased communication and that a single-bit error can destroy the integrity of a process, digital computation is doomed—or so it seemed at the time.

Remarkably, that was the common view until Shannon came along with the first key idea of the information age. He demonstrated how we can create arbitrarily accurate communication using the most unreliable communication channels. What Shannon said in his now landmark paper, "A Mathematical Theory of Communication," published in the *Bell System Technical Journal* in July and October 1948, and in particular in his noisy-channel coding theorem, was that if you have available a channel with any error rate (except for exactly 50 percent per bit, which would mean that channel is transmitting pure noise), you are able to transmit a message and make the error rate as accurate as you want. In other words, the error rate can be one bit out of n bits, where n can be as large as you want. So, for example, in the extreme, if you have a channel that transmits bits of information correctly only 51 percent of the time (that is, it transmits the correct bit just slightly more often than the wrong bit), you can nonetheless transmit messages such that only one bit out of a million is incorrect, or one bit out of a trillion or a trillion trillion.

How is this possible? The answer is through redundancy.

That may seem obvious now, but it was not obvious at the time. As a simple example, if I transmit each bit three times and take the majority vote, I will have substantially increased the reliability of the result. If that is not good enough, increase the redundancy until you get the reliability you need. The idea of simply repeating information is the easiest way to see how we can achieve arbitrarily high accuracy rates from low-accuracy channels, but this approach is not the most efficient approach. Shannon's paper established the field of information theory and presented optimal methods of error detection and correction codes that can achieve any target accuracy through any nonrandom channel.

Older readers will recall telephone modems that transmitted information through noisy analog phone lines, which included audible hisses and pops and many other forms of distortion, but nonetheless were able to transmit digital data with very high accuracy rates, thanks to Shannon's noisy-channel theorem.

The same issue and the same solution exist for digital memory. Ever wonder how CDs, DVDs, and program disks continue to provide reliable results even after the disk has been dropped on the floor and scratched? Again, we can thank Shannon. Computation consists of three elements: communication (which, as I mentioned, is pervasive both within and between computers), memory, and logic gates (which perform the arithmetic and logical functions). The accuracy of logic gates can also be made arbitrarily high by similarly using error detection and correction codes. It is due to Shannon's theorem that we can handle arbitrarily large and complex digital data and algorithms without the processes being disturbed or destroyed by errors.

The second important idea on which the information age relies is the universality of computation. In 1936 Alan Turing described his "Turing machine," which is not an actual machine but a thought experiment. His theoretical computer consists of an infinitely long memory tape with a 1 or a 0 in each square. Input to the machine is presented on this tape. The machine reads the tape one square at a time. The machine also contains a table of rules, essentially a stored program. The rules consist of numbered states. Each rule specifies one action if the square currently being read is a 0 and a different action if the current square is a 1. Possible actions include writing a 0 or a 1 on the tape, moving the tape one square to the right or the left, or halting. Each state then specifies the number of the next state that the machine should be in. When the machine halts, it has completed its algorithm, and the output of the process is left on the tape. Even though the tape is theoretically infinite in length, any actual program (that does not get into an infinite loop) uses only a finite portion of the tape, so if we limit ourselves to a finite memory, the machine still solves a useful set of problems.

If the Turing machine sounds simple, that was Turing's objective. He wanted his Turing machine to be as simple as possible (but no simpler, to paraphrase Einstein). Turing and Alonzo Church, his former professor, went on to develop the Church-Turing thesis, which states that if a problem that can be presented to a Turing machine is not solvable by a Turing machine, it is also not solvable by *any* machine, following natural law. Even though the Turing machine has only a handful of commands and processes only one bit at a time, it can compute anything that any computer can compute.

"Strong" interpretations of the Church-Turing thesis propose an essential equivalence between what a human can think or know and what is computable by a machine. The basic idea is that the human brain is subject to natural law, and thus its information-processing ability cannot exceed that of a machine (and therefore of a Turing machine).

We can properly credit Turing with establishing the theoretical foundation of computation with his 1936 paper, but it is important to note that Turing was deeply influenced by a lecture that John von Neumann gave in Cambridge, England, in 1935 on his stored-program concept, a concept enshrined in the Turing machine. In turn, von Neumann was influenced by Turing's 1936 paper, which elegantly laid out the principles of computation, and he made it required reading for his colleagues in the late 1930s and early 1940s.

In the same paper, Turing reports another unexpected discovery, that of unsolvable problems. These are problems that are well defined and have unique answers that can be shown to exist but that we can also prove can never be computed by a Turing machine—that is to say, by *any* machine—which is a reversal of what had been a nineteenth-century confidence that problems that could be defined would ultimately be solved. Turing showed that there are as many unsolvable problems as solvable ones. Kurt Gödel reached a similar conclusion in his 1931 "Incompleteness Theorem." We are thus left with the perplexing situation of being able to define a problem, to prove that a unique answer exists, and yet to know that the answer can never be discovered.

A lot more can be said about the philosophical implications of the work of Turing, Church, and Gödel, but for the purposes of this foreword, it is sufficient to say that Turing showed that computation is essentially based on a very simple mechanism. Because the Turing machine (and, therefore, any computer) is capable of basing its future course of action on results it has already computed, it is capable of making decisions and modeling arbitrarily complex hierarchies of information.

Turing designed and completed what is arguably the first computer, called the Colossus, by December 1943 to decode messages that had been encrypted by the Nazi Enigma coding machine. It was designed for one task and could not be reprogrammed for a different task. But it performed this one task brilliantly and is credited with enabling the Allies to overcome the 3:1 advantage that the German Luftwaffe enjoyed over the British Royal Air Force, enabling the Allies to win the crucial Battle of Britain.

It was on these foundations that John von Neumann created the architecture of the modern computer, the von Neumann machine, which has remained the core structure of
essentially every computer for the past sixty-six years, from
the microcontroller in your washing machine to the largest
supercomputers. This is the third key idea of the information age. In a paper dated June 30, 1945, titled "First Draft
of a Report on the EDVAC," von Neumann presented the
concepts that have dominated computation ever since. The
von Neumann model includes a central processing unit
where arithmetical and logical operations are carried out, a
memory unit where the program and data are stored, mass
storage, a program counter, and input/output channels.
This conception is described in the first half of this book.
Although von Neumann's paper was intended as an internal
project document, it became the Bible for computer designers in the 1940s and 1950s and, indeed, has influenced
the building of every computer since that time.

The Turing machine was not designed to be practical.
Turing's theorems were not concerned with the efficiency of
solving problems but rather with examining the range of
problems that could be solved by computation. Von Neumann's goal was to create a practical concept of a computational machine. His concept replaces Turing's one-bit computations with multiple-bit words (generally some multiple
of eight bits). Turing's memory tape is sequential, so Turing
machine programs spend an inordinate amount of time

moving the tape back and forth to store and retrieve intermediate results. In contrast, von Neumann's machine has a random access memory, so any data item can be immediately retrieved.

One of von Neumann's key concepts is the stored program, which he had introduced a decade earlier: the program is stored in the same type of random access memory as the data (and often in the same block of memory). This allows the computer to be reprogrammed for different tasks. It even allows for self-modifying code (if the program store is writable), which allows for a powerful form of recursion. Up until that time, virtually all computers, including Turing's own Colossus, were built for a specific task. The stored program allows a computer to be truly universal, thereby fulfilling Turing's vision of the universality of computation.

Another of von Neumann's key concepts is for each instruction to include an operation code specifying the arithmetic or logical operation to be performed and the address of an operand from memory. Von Neumann's formulation was introduced with his publication of the design of the EDVAC, a project he conducted with collaborators J. Presper Eckert and John Mauchly. The EDVAC itself did not actually run until 1951, by which time there were other stored-program computers, such as the Manchester Small-Scale Experimental Machine, ENIAC, EDSAC, and BINAC, all of which had been deeply influenced by von Neumann's paper and involved Eckert and Mauchly as designers. Von Neumann was a direct contributor to the design of a number of these machines, including a later version of ENIAC which supported a stored program.

There were a few precursors to von Neumann's architecture, although none were true von Neumann machines, with one surprising exception. Howard Aiken's Mark I, built in 1944, had an element of programmability but did not use a stored program. It read instructions from a punched paper tape and then executed each command immediately. There was no conditional branch instruction, so it cannot be considered to be an example of von Neumann architecture.

Predating the Mark I was the creation of the Z-3 computer in 1941 by Konrad Zuse. It also read its program from a tape (in this case, coded on film) and also lacked a conditional branch instruction. Interestingly, Zuse had support from the German Aircraft Research Institute which used the Z-3 to study wing flutter, but his proposal to the Nazi government for funding to replace his relays with vacuum tubes was turned down. The Nazis deemed computation as "not war important."

The one true precursor to von Neumann's concept came a full century earlier. Charles Babbage's Analytical Engine, which he first described in 1837, incorporated the idea of a stored program, which it provided via punched cards borrowed from the Jacquard loom. Its random access memory included one thousand words of 50 decimal digits each (the equivalent of about 21 kilobytes). Each instruction included an operation code and an operand number, just like modern machine languages. It also included conditional branching and looping, so it was a true von Neumann machine. It appears that the Analytical Engine was beyond Babbage's mechanical and organizational skills, and it never ran. It is unclear whether the twentieth-century pioneers of the computer, including von Neumann, were aware of Babbage's work.

Despite never running, Babbage's computer resulted in the creation of the field of software programming. Ada Byron, Countess of Lovelace and the only legitimate child of the poet Lord Byron, wrote programs for the Analytical Engine that she needed to debug in her own mind, a practice well known to software engineers today as "table checking." She translated an article by the Italian mathematician Luigi Menabrea on the Analytical Engine and added extensive notes of her own. She wrote that "the Analytical Engine weaves algebraic patterns, just as the Jacquard loom weaves flowers and leaves." She went on to provide perhaps the first speculations on the feasibility of artificial intelligence, but concluded that the Analytical Engine had "no pretensions whatever to originate anything."

Babbage's conception is quite miraculous when you consider the era in which he lived and worked. However, by the mid-twentieth century, his work had been lost in the mists of time. It was von Neumann who conceptualized and articulated the key principles of the computer as we know it today, and the world recognizes this by continuing to refer to the von Neumann machine as the principal model of computation.

Keep in mind that the von Neumann machine continually communicates data between and within its various units, so it would not be possible to build one if it were not for Shannon's theorems and the methods he devised for transmitting and storing reliable digital information.

That brings us to the fourth important idea, which is to find ways to endow computers with intelligence, to go beyond Ada Byron's conclusion that a computer cannot think creatively. Alan Turing had already introduced this goal with his 1950 paper, "Computing Machinery and Intelligence," which includes his now famous "Turing test" for ascertaining whether or not an AI has achieved a human level of intelligence. In this book, after introducing von Neumann architecture, von Neumann looks to the human brain itself. The human brain is, after all, the best example we have of an intelligent system. If we can learn its methods, we can use these biologically inspired paradigms to build more intelligent machines. This book is the earliest serious examination of the human brain from the perspective of a mathematician and computer pioneer. Prior to von Neumann, the fields of computer science and neuroscience were two islands with no bridge between them.

It is ironic that the last work of one of the most brilliant mathematicians of the twentieth century and one of the pioneers of the computer age was an examination of intelligence itself. The work was intended as a series of lectures for Yale University, but because of the ravages of cancer, von Neumann never delivered the lectures and did not complete the manuscript from which the lectures were to be given. It nonetheless remains a brilliant and prophetic foreshadowing of what I regard as humanity's most daunting and important project.

Von Neumann starts by articulating the differences and similarities between the computer and the human brain. Given that he wrote in 1955 and 1956, the manuscript is remarkably accurate, especially in the details that are pertinent to the comparison. He notes that the output of neurons is digital: an axon either fires or it doesn't. This was far from obvious at the time, in that the output could have been an analog signal. The processing in the dendrites leading into a neuron and in the soma neuron cell body, however, are analog. He describes these calculations as a weighted sum of inputs with a threshold. This model of how neurons work led to the field of connectionism, in which systems are built based on this neuron model in both hardware and software. The first such connectionist system was created by Frank Rosenblatt as a software program on an IBM 704 computer at Cornell in 1957.

We now have more sophisticated models of how neurons combine inputs, but the essential idea of analog processing of dendrite inputs using neurotransmitter concentrations has held up. We would not have expected von Neumann to get all of the details of how neurons process information correct in 1956, but the key points on which he bases his arguments remain valid.

Von Neumann applies the concept of the universality of computation to conclude that even though the architecture and building blocks of the brain and the computer appear to be radically different, we can nonetheless conclude that a von Neumann machine can simulate a brain's processing. The converse does not hold, however, because the brain is not a von Neumann machine and does not have a stored program as such. Its algorithm, or methods, are implicit in its structure.

Von Neumann correctly concludes that neurons can learn patterns from their inputs, which we now know are coded in neurotransmitter concentrations. What was not known in von Neumann's time is that learning also takes place through the creation and destruction of connections between neurons.

Von Neumann notes that the speed of neural processing is extremely slow, on the order of a hundred calculations per second, but that the brain compensates for this through massive parallel processing. Each one of its 10^{10} neurons is processing simultaneously (this number is also reasonably accurate; estimates today are between 10^{10} and 10^{11}). In fact, each of the connections (with an average of about 10^3 connections per neuron) is computing simultaneously.

His estimates and description of neural processing are remarkable, given the primitive state of neuroscience at the time. One description that I disagree with is von Neumann's estimate of the brain's memory capacity. He assumes that the brain remembers every input for an entire lifetime. Sixty years is about 2×10^9 seconds. With about fourteen inputs to each neuron per second (which is actually low by at least three orders of magnitude), and with 10^{10} neurons, he gets an estimate of about 10^{20} bits for the brain's memory capacity. The reality is that we remember only a very small fraction of our thoughts and experiences, and these memories are not stored as bit patterns at a low level (such as a video image), but rather as sequences of higher-level patterns. Our cortex is organized as a hierarchy of pattern recognizers. Some of these recognizers will recognize certain topological forms, such as the cross bar in a capital "A" or its lower concavity. These low-level recognizers in the neocortex feed those recognitions to pattern recognizers at a higher level. At that next level, recognizers may recognize specific printed letters such as the letter "A." At an even higher level, words may be recognized, such as the word "Apple." In another portion of the cortex, a recognizer at a comparable level may recognize the object, an apple; and in yet another portion, a recognizer may recognize the spoken word, "apple." At a much higher conceptual level, a recognizer may conclude, "That was funny." Our memory of events and thoughts is coded in terms of these higher-level recognitions. If we recall a memory of an experience, there is nothing equivalent to a video playing in our head. Rather, we recall a sequence of these high-level patterns. We have to reimagine the experience, for the details are not explicitly remembered.

You can demonstrate this to yourself by trying to recall a recent experience—for example, the last time you took a walk. How much of that experience do you remember? Who was the fifth person you encountered? Did you see a baby carriage? A mailbox? What did you see when you turned the first corner? If you passed some stores, what was in the second window? Perhaps you can reconstruct the answers to these questions from the few cues that you remember, but most of us do not have perfect recall of our experiences. Machines can, in fact, recall easily, and that is one advantage of artificial intelligence.

There are very few discussions in this book that I find to be at significant odds with what we now understand. We are not in a position today to describe the brain perfectly, so we would not expect a book from 1956 on reverse engineering the brain to do so. That being said, von Neumann's descriptions are remarkably up to date, and the details on which he bases his conclusions remain valid. As he describes each mechanism in the brain, he shows how a modern computer could accomplish the same operation, despite the apparent differences. The brain's analog mechanisms can be simulated through digital ones because digital computation can emulate analog values to any desired degree of precision (and the precision of analog information in the brain is quite low).

The brain's massive parallelism can also be simulated, given the significant speed advantage of computers in serial computation (an advantage that has vastly expanded since the book was written). In addition, we can also use parallel processing in computers by using parallel von Neumann machines. That is exactly how supercomputers work today.

Considering how quickly we are able to make decisions and how very slowly neurons compute, he concludes that the brain's methods cannot involve lengthy sequential algorithms. When a baseball fielder on third base decides to throw to first rather than to second base, he makes this decision in a fraction of a second. There is time for each neuron to go through only a handful of cycles (the period of time necessary for neural circuits to consider new inputs). Von Neumann correctly concludes that the brain's remarkable powers come from the ten billion neurons being able to process information all at the same time. Recent advances in reverse engineering the visual cortex have confirmed that we make sophisticated visual judgments in only three or four neural cycles.

There is considerable plasticity in the brain, which enables us to learn. But there is far greater plasticity in a computer, which can completely restructure its methods by changing its software. Thus a computer will be able to emulate the brain, but the converse is not the case.

When von Neumann compared the capacity of the brain's massively parallel organization to the (few) computers of his time, it was clear that the brain had far greater capacity than computers circa 1956. Today the first supercomputers are being built that achieve a speed matching some of the more conservative estimates of the speed required to functionally simulate the human brain (about 10^{16} operations per second). I estimate that the hardware for this level of computation will cost $1,000 early in the 2020s. Even though it was remarkably early in the history of the computer when this manuscript was written, von Neumann nonetheless had confidence that both the hardware and the software of human intelligence would ultimately be available. That was the reason he prepared these lectures.

Von Neumann was deeply aware of the accelerating pace of progress and the profound implications of this progression for humanity's future, which brings us to the fifth key idea of the information age. A year after von Neumann's death in 1957, fellow mathematician Stan Ulam quoted von Neumann as having said that "the ever accelerating progress of technology and changes in the mode of human life give the appearance of approaching some essential singularity in the history of the race beyond which human affairs, as we know them, could not continue." This is the first known use of the word "singularity" in the context of human history.

Ray Kurzweil

Further Readings

Bochner, S. (1958). *A Biographical Memoir of John von Neumann*. Washington, D.C.: National Academy of Sciences.

Turing, A. M. (1936). "On Computable Numbers, with an Application to the Entscheidungsproblem." *Proceedings of the London Mathematical Society* 42: 230–65. doi:10.1112/plms/s2-42.1.230.

Turing, A. M. (1938). "On Computable Numbers, with an Application to the Entscheidungsproblem: A Correction." *Proceedings of the London Mathematical Society* 43: 544–46. doi:10.1112/plms/s2-43.6.544.

Turing, A. M. (October 1950). "Computing Machinery and Intelligence." *Mind* 59 (236): 433–60.

Ulam, S. (May 1958). "Tribute to John von Neumann." *Bulletin of the American Mathematical Society* 64 (3, part 2): 1–49.

von Neumann, John. (June 30, 1945). "First Draft of a Report on the EDVAC." Moore School of Electrical Engineering, University of Pennsylvania.

von Neumann, John. (July and October 1948). "A Mathematical Theory of Communication." *Bell System Technical Journal* 27.

FOREWORD TO THE SECOND EDITION

This innocent-looking little book lies at the eye of a hurricane. It represents a locus of clarity and calm at the center of a vast vortex of powerful arguments and competing research programs. And it is all the more singular for having been written in 1956, at the very beginning of the recent explosion in electronic computer technology, an explosion that will forever define the second half of the twentieth century. What John von Neumann attempted to provide in his final lecture series—here published as a single book— was a balanced assessment of the brain's possible computational activities, seen through the lens of modern computational theory and in the light of computer technology and empirical neuroscience as they existed in that period.

One might expect that any such assessment, made at that time, must now be hopelessly dated. But in fact the opposite is true. On the side of pure computational theory (the theory of generating the elements of any computable function), the foundations laid by William Church, Alan Turing, and, to a degree, von Neumann himself have proved as sturdy and as fertile as any of them could have hoped. That lens was well turned at the start, and it still provides a sharp focus on a wide range of problems.

On the side of computer technology, the turn-of-the-millennium machines that now grace every office and half the homes in America are all instances of what has come to be called the "von Neumann architecture." They are all examples of a functional organization developed and explored primarily by von Neumann, an organization that uses a sequential "program" held in the machine's modifiable "memory" to dictate the nature and the order of the basic computational steps carried out by the machine's "central processor." The original rationale for that organization is here briskly and lucidly outlined in von Neumann's own words, although he speaks of "code" where we now speak of "programs," and he speaks of "complete codes" versus "short codes" where we now speak of "machine-language programs" versus "high-level programming languages." But only the words, and the clock-speeds of the machines, have changed. John von Neumann would recognize every machine currently in sight—from PalmPilot organizers to supercomputers, whether running poker games or galactic-genesis simulations—as a further instance of his original architectural vision. He has in no relevant sense been left behind by our many advances in computer technology.

On the side of empirical neuroscience, the situation is rather more complicated but even more interesting. To begin with, the several neurosciences (neuroanatomy, neurophysiology, developmental neurobiology, and cognitive neurobiology) have all made monumental advances themselves. Here, too, a half-century's painstaking research has produced a substantially new science. Thanks to many recent experimental techniques (such as electron and confocal microscopy, patch clamping, electro- and magneto-encephalography, CAT scans, PET scans, and MRI scans), we now have a much better picture of the brain's filamentary microstructure, the electrochemical behavior of its microscopic parts, and its global activities during various forms of conscious cognition. Though still the home of many mysteries, the brain is no longer the "black box" it used to be.

Curiously, however, these two kindred sciences—one focused on *artificial* cognitive processes and the other on *natural* cognitive processes—pursued their parallel concerns in substantial isolation from each other, from the 1950s right through to the present. The people who earned advanced degrees in computer science typically learned little or (more often) nothing about the biological brain, and their research activities were typically focused on writing programs, developing new languages, or developing and producing everbetter microchip hardwares, none of which brought them into contact with the empirical neurosciences. Equally, the people who earned advanced degrees in neuroscience typically learned little or nothing about computational theory, automata theory, formal logic and binary arithmetic, or the electronics of transistors. More likely, they spent their research time staining slices of brain tissue for microscopic examination or putting microelectrodes into living neurons to record their electrical behaviors during various cognitive tasks. If they did use a computer and learn a programming language—as many did—they used it only as a tool to direct and collate their experimental activities, as one might use a voltmeter, a calculator, or a filing cabinet.

The truth, it now seems, is that, while each of these two sciences has a great deal to learn about its own domain, and each was indeed a roaring success, neither science had much to teach the other about the other's own domain. Despite the presumptive overlap—they shared a concern with cognitive or computational processes, after all—they flowed in parallel streams and each made its remarkable progress with little or no input from the sister science. But why?

A persistently recurring answer is that the biological brain has a physical organization and uses a computational strategy that is very different from the von Neumann architecture used in standard computing machines. For close to fifty years, the two sister sciences have in fact been focused on importantly different subject matters. In retrospect, it is no wonder that they developed in substantial independence of one another.

This answer is still fiercely disputed, and it may, indeed, be mistaken. But it lies at the heart of current discussions about how the *biological* brain actually performs its many cognitive miracles and how best to pursue the still vital enterprise of constructing various forms of *artificial* intelligence. Should we simply press past the obvious limitations of biological systems (limitations mostly of speed and reliability) and pursue the dazzling potential of electronic systems, systems that can, in principle and even with a von Neumann architecture, implement or simulate *any* possible computational activities? Or should we attempt instead, for whatever reasons, to mimic the computational organization displayed in the brains of insects, fishes, birds, and mammals? And what organization is that, anyway? Is it importantly or interestingly different from what goes on in our artificial machines?

Here, the reader may be surprised to discover, John von Neumann weighs in with a prescient, powerful, and decidedly nonclassical answer. He spends the first half of the book leading the reader stepwise through the classical conceptions for which he is so famously responsible, and as he turns finally to address the brain, he hazards the initial conclusion that "its functioning is *prima facie* digital." But this initial take on the neuronal data is also prima facie procrustean, a fact that von Neumann acknowledges immediately and subsequently turns to pursue at length.

The first problem he notes is that the connections between neurons do not show the telltale "two lines in and one line out" configuration that classical *and*-gates and *or*-gates display. Though each cell typically projects exactly one output axon, as the classical take would require, each cell *receives* more than a hundred, even more than several thousand, inputs from many other neurons. This fact is not decisive—there are, for example, multivalent logics. But it does give him pause.

The plot thickens as von Neumann pursues a point-by-point comparison between the fundamental dimensions of the brain's "basic active organs" (presumptively, the neurons) and the computer's "basic active organs" (the various logic gates). Spatially, he observes, neurons have the advantage of being at least 10^2 times smaller than their presumptive electronic counterparts. (At the time, this estimate was exactly right, but with the unforeseen advent of photo-etched microchips, this size advantage has simply disappeared, at least where two-dimensional sheets are concerned. We can forgive von Neumann this one.)

More important, neurons have a major disadvantage where the speed of their operations is concerned. Neurons are, he estimates, perhaps 10^5 times slower than vacuum tubes or transistors in the time required to complete a basic logical operation. Here he is portentously correct, in ways about to emerge. If anything, he underestimates the neuron's very considerable disadvantage. If we assume that a neuron can have a "clock frequency" of no better than roughly 10^2 Hz, then the clock frequencies of almost 1,000 MHz (that is, 10^9 basic operations per second) now displayed in the most recent generation of desktop machines push the neuron's disadvantage closer to a factor of 10^7. The conclusion is inescapable. If the brain is a digital computer with a von Neumann architecture, it is doomed to be a computational tortoise by comparison.

Additionally, the accuracy with which the biological brain can represent any variable is also many orders of magnitude below the accuracies available to a digital computer. Computers, von Neumann observes, can easily use and manipulate eight, ten, or twelve decimal places of representation, while the neuron's presumed mode of representation—the frequency of the spike train it sends down its axon—appears limited to a representational accuracy of at most two decimal places (specifically, plus or minus perhaps 1 percent of a frequency maximum of roughly 100 Hz). This is troubling because, in the course of any computation that involves a great many steps, small errors of representation in the early steps regularly accumulate into larger errors at the closing steps. Worse, he adds, for many important classes of computation, even tiny errors in the early steps get exponentially *amplified* in subsequent steps, which inevitably leads to wildly inaccurate final outputs. Thus, if the brain is a digital computer with only two decimal places of representational accuracy, it is doomed to be a computational dunce.

Conjointly, these two severe limitations—one on speed, and the other on accuracy—drive von Neumann to the conclusion that whatever computational regime the brain is using, it must be one that somehow involves a minimum of what he calls "logical depth." That is, whatever the brain is doing, it cannot be sequentially performing thousands upon thousands of sequentially orchestrated computational steps, as in the super-high frequency, recursive activity of a digital machine's central processor. Given the slowness of its neuronal activities, there isn't enough time for the brain to complete any but the most trivial of computations. And given the low accuracy of its typical representations, it would be computationally incompetent even if it did have enough time.

This is a poignant conclusion for von Neumann to have reached because it is obvious that, despite the preceding limitations, the brain somehow manages to perform a great variety of sophisticated computations, and it does so, moreover, in the twinkling of an eye. But there is nothing wrong with his arguments. The limitations he points to are entirely genuine. What, then, are we to make of the brain?

As von Neumann correctly perceives, the brain's computational regime appears to compensate for its inescapable lack of logical depth by exploiting an extraordinary logical breadth. As he says, "large and efficient natural automata are likely to be highly *parallel*, while large and efficient artificial automata will tend to be less so, and rather to be serial" (emphasis his). The former "will tend to pick up as many logical (or informational) items as possible *simultaneously*, and process them *simultaneously*" (emphasis ours). This means, he adds, that we must reach out, beyond the brain's neurons, to include all of its many *synapses* in our all-up count of the brain's "basic active organs."

These are all major insights. As we now know, the brain contains roughly 10^{14} synaptic connections, each of which modulates the arriving axonal signal before passing it on to the receiving neuron. The job of the neuron is then to sum, or otherwise integrate, the inputs from those synaptic connections (as many as 10,000 onto a single cell) and generate its own axonal output in turn. Most important, these tiny modulatory actions all take place simultaneously. This means that, with each synapse being active perhaps 100 times per second (recall that typical spiking frequencies are in the range of 100 Hz), the total number of basic information-processing actions performed by the brain must be roughly 10^2 times 10^{14}, or 10^{16} operations per second! This is a striking achievement for any system, and it compares very favorably with our earlier count of 10^9 basic operations per second for a cutting-edge desktop machine. The brain is neither a tortoise nor a dunce after all, for it was never a serial, digital machine to begin with: it is a massively parallel analog machine.

This much von Neumann suggests herein, and modern neuroscience and the computer modeling of parallel networks tend strongly to confirm it. The alternative computational strategy on which von Neumann speculated now appears to be an instance of the simultaneous *multiplication* of each of many thousands or millions of simultaneous axonal spiking frequencies (which constitute a very large input vector) by the coefficients of an even larger matrix (namely, the configuration of the many millions of synaptic junctions that connect one neuronal population to the next) to produce an output vector (namely, a new and different pattern of simultaneous spiking frequencies across the receiving population of neurons). It is the acquired global configuration of those many millions, nay trillions, of synaptic connections that embodies whatever knowledge and skills the brain may have acquired. And it is those same synaptic connections that so swiftly perform the computational transformations upon any axonal inputs—from the senses, for example—that arrive at their collective doorstep. This yields both the speed and the freedom from recursively amplified errors that von Neumann deemed essential.

It must quickly be said, however, that this decisive insight does nothing to dim the integrity of his digital and serial technologies, nor does it dim our hopes for creating artificial intelligence. Quite the contrary. We can make electronic versions of synaptic connections, and, eschewing the classical von Neumann architecture, we can create vast parallel networks of artificial neurons, thus realizing electronic versions of the "shallow-depth" but "extraordinary-breadth" computational regime evidently exploited by the brain. These will have the additional and most intriguing property of being roughly 10^6 times faster, overall, than their biological namesakes, simply because they will have electronic rather than biochemical components. This means many things. For one, a synapse-for-synapse *electronic* duplicate of your biological brain could enjoy, in only thirty seconds, a train of thought that would consume a year's time as conducted by the components within your own skull. And that same machine could enjoy, in half an hour, an intellectual life that would consume your entire three-score-and-ten years, if conducted within your own brain. Intelligence, clearly, has an interesting future.

A note of caution must here be sounded. It is true that smallish artificial neural networks have already been constructed on the assumption that synapses are tiny multipliers, that neurons are tiny summators with a sigmoid output function, and that information is coded solely in the frequency of neuronal spiking. And it is true that many of these networks display remarkable "cognitive" talents, at least after lengthy training. But these same network models, analog and massively parallel though they may be, exhibit little of the subtlety and variety displayed in the behavior of real synapses and real neurons. Unfolding neuroscientific research continues to teach us, just as it taught von Neumann, that our first-pass models of brain activity are, at best, crude approximations of the neurocomputational reality, and they may turn out to be just as mistaken as the historical guess—here challenged by von Neumann—that the brain's operations are primarily digital. There is more than one way to code information in an axon's behavior;

there is more than one way to modulate it at a synapse; and there is more than one way to integrate it within a neuron. Our current models function well enough to capture our imaginations, but the brain still harbors many puzzles, and it portends major surprises yet to come. Our business here is far from done, and we must be as humble before the empirical facts as von Neumann evidently was.

Von Neumann is responsible for the computational architecture that underlies almost all of the twentieth century's "computer revolution," a revolution that will have an impact on humanity's long-term future at least as great as Isaac Newton's mechanics or James Maxwell's electromagnetics. Moreover, von Neumann had the character and the insight, where the biological brain is concerned, to see past his own computational architecture to the outlines of a new explanatory paradigm of perhaps even greater power.

At the end of broad discussions on the nature of intelligence, one often hears a commentator call out, in hope, for the arrival of someone to serve as "the Newton of the mind." We wish to end on a different note. As the preceding commentary suggests, and as the following book illustrates, there is a strong case to be made that the hoped-for Newton has already come and, alas, already gone. His name is John von Neumann.

Paul and Patricia Churchland

PREFACE

To give the Silliman Lectures, one of the oldest and most outstanding academic lecture series in the United States, is considered a privilege and an honor among scholars all over the world. Traditionally the lecturer is asked to give a series of talks, over a period of about two weeks, and then to shape the manuscript of the lectures into a book to be published under the auspices of Yale University, the home and headquarters of the Silliman Lectures.

Early in 1955 my husband, John von Neumann, was invited by Yale University to give the Silliman Lectures during the spring term of 1956, some time in late March or early April. Johnny was deeply honored and gratified by this invitation, despite the fact that he had to make his acceptance subject to one condition—namely, that the lectures be limited to one week only. The accompanying manuscript would, however, cover more fully his chosen topic—The Computer and the Brain—a theme in which he had been interested for a considerable time. The request to abbreviate the lecture period was made of necessity, as he had just been appointed by President Eisenhower as one of the members of the Atomic Energy Commission, a full-time job which does not permit even a scientist much time away from his desk in Washington. My husband knew, however, that he could find time to write the lectures, for he had always done his writing at home during the night or at dawn. His capacity for work was practically unlimited, particularly if he was interested, and the many unexplored possibilities of automata did interest him very much indeed; so he felt quite confident that he could prepare a full manuscript even though the lecture period would have to be somewhat cut. Yale University, helpful and understanding at this early period as well as later, when there was only sadness, sorrow, and need, accepted this arrangement, and Johnny started his new job at the Commission with the added incentive that he would continue his work on the theory of automata even if it was done a little *en cache*.

In the spring of 1955 we moved from Princeton to Washington, and Johnny went on leave of absence from the Institute for Advanced Study, where he had been Professor in the School of Mathematics since 1933.

Johnny was born in Budapest, Hungary, in 1903. Even in his early years he had shown a remarkable ability and interest in scientific matters, and as a child his almost photographic memory manifested itself in many unusual ways. Reaching college age, he studied first chemistry and then mathematics at the University of Berlin, the Technische Hochschule in

Zurich, and the University of Budapest. In 1927 he was appointed Privatdozent at the University of Berlin, probably one of the youngest persons appointed to such a position in any of the German universities within the last few decades. Later Johnny taught at the University of Hamburg, and in 1930, for the first time, crossed the Atlantic, having accepted the invitation of Princeton University to become a guest lecturer for one year. In 1931 he became a member of the faculty of Princeton University, thus making his permanent home in the United States and becoming a citizen of the New World. During the 1920's and 30's Johnny's scientific interest was ranging widely, mostly in theoretical fields. His publications included works on quantum theory, mathematical logic, ergodic theory, continuous geometry, problems dealing with rings of operators, and many other areas of pure mathematics. Then, during the late thirties, he became interested in questions of theoretical hydrodynamics, particularly in the great difficulties encountered in obtaining solutions to partial differential equations by known analytical methods. This endeavor, carried forward when war clouds were darkening the horizon all over the world, brought him into scientific defense work and made him more and more interested in the applied fields of mathematics and physics. The interaction of shock waves, a very intricate hydrodynamic problem, became one of the important defense research interests, and the tremendous amount of calculations required to get some of the answers motivated

Johnny to employ a high-speed computing machine for this purpose. The ENIAC, built in Philadelphia for the Ballistic Research Laboratories of Army Ordnance, was Johnny's first introduction to the vast possibilities of solving many yet unresolved questions with the aid of automation. He helped to modify some of the mathematical-logical design of the ENIAC, and from then until his last conscious hours, he remained interested in and intrigued by the still unexplored aspects and possibilities of the fast-growing use of automata.

In 1943, soon after the Manhattan Project was started, Johnny became one of the scientists who "disappeared into the West," commuting back and forth between Washington, Los Alamos, and many other places. This was the period during which he became completely convinced, and tried to convince others in many varied fields, that numerical calculations done on fast electronic computing devices would substantially facilitate the solution of many difficult, unsolved, scientific problems.

After the war, together with a small group of selected engineers and mathematicians, Johnny built, at the Institute for Advanced Study, an experimental electronic calculator, popularly known as the JONIAC, which eventually became the pilot model for similar machines all over the country. Some of the basic principles developed in the JONIAC are used even today in the fastest and most modern calculators. To design the machine, Johnny and his co-workers tried to imitate some of the known operations of the live brain. This is the aspect which led him to study neurology, to seek out men in the fields of neurology and psychiatry, to attend many meetings on these subjects, and, eventually, to give lectures to such groups on the possibilities of copying an extremely simplified model of the living brain for man-made machines. In the Silliman Lectures these thoughts were to be further developed and expanded.

During the postwar years Johnny divided his work among scientific problems in various fields. Particularly, he became interested in meteorology, where numerical calculations seemed to be helpful in opening entirely new vistas; part of his time was spent helping to make calculations in the ever-expanding problems of nuclear physics. He continued to work closely with the laboratories of the Atomic Energy Commission, and in 1952 he became a member of the General Advisory Committee to the AEC.

On March 15, 1955, Johnny was sworn in as a member of the Atomic Energy Commission, and early in May we moved our household to Washington. Three months later, in August, the pattern of our active and exciting life, centered around my husband's indefatigable and astounding mind, came to an abrupt stop; Johnny had developed severe pains in his left shoulder, and after surgery, bone cancer was diagnosed. The ensuing months were of alternating hope and despair; sometimes we were confident that the lesion in the shoulder was a single manifestation of the dread disease, not to recur for a long time, but then indefinable aches and pains that he suffered from at times dashed our hopes for the future. Throughout this period Johnny worked feverishly—during the day in his office or making the many trips required by the job; at night on scientific papers, things which he had postponed until he would be through with his term at the Commission. He now started to work systematically on the manuscript for the Silliman Lectures; most of what is written in the following pages was produced in those days of uncertainty and waiting. In late November the next blow came: several lesions were found on his spine, and he developed serious difficulties in walking. From then on, everything went from bad to worse, though still there was some hope left that with treatment and care the fatal illness might be arrested, for a while at least.

By January 1956 Johnny was confined to a wheelchair, but still he attended meetings, was wheeled into his office, and continued working on the manuscript for the lecture. Clearly his strength was waning from day to day; all trips and speaking engagements had to be canceled one by one, with this single exception—the Silliman Lectures. There was some hope that with X-ray treatments the spine might be, at least temporarily, sufficiently strengthened by late March to permit his traveling to New Haven and fulfilling this one obligation that meant so very much to him. Even so, the Silliman Lecture Committee had to be asked further to reduce the lectures to one or two at the most, for the strain of a whole week of lecturing would have been dangerous in his weakened condition. By March, however, all false hopes were gone, and there was no longer any question of Johnny being able to travel anywhere. Again Yale University, as helpful and understanding as ever, did not cancel the lectures, but suggested that if the manuscript could be delivered, someone else would read it for him. In spite of many efforts, Johnny could not finish writing his planned lectures in time; as a matter of tragic fate he could never finish writing them at all.

In early April Johnny was admitted to Walter Reed Hospital; he never left the hospital grounds again until his death on February 8, 1957. The unfinished manuscript of the Silliman Lectures went with him to the hospital, where he made a few more attempts to work on it; but by then the illness had definitely gained the upper hand, and even Johnny's exceptional mind could not overcome the weariness of the body.

I should like to be permitted to express my deep gratitude to the Silliman Lecture Committee, to Yale University, and to the Yale University Press, all of which have been so helpful and kind during the last, sad years of Johnny's life and now honor his memory by admitting his unfinished and fragmentary manuscript to the series of the Silliman Lectures Publications.

Klara von Neumann
Washington, D.C., September 1957

INTRODUCTION

Since I am neither a neurologist nor a psychiatrist, but a mathematician, the work that follows requires some explanation and justification. It is an approach toward the understanding of the nervous system from the mathematician's point of view. However, this statement must immediately be qualified in both of its essential parts.

First, it is an overstatement to describe what I am attempting here as an "approach toward the understanding"; it is merely a somewhat systematized set of speculations as to how such an approach ought to be made. That is, I am trying to guess which of the—mathematically guided—lines of attack seem, from the hazy distance in which we see most of them, a priori promising, and which ones have the opposite appearance. I will also offer some rationalizations of these guesses.

Second, the "mathematician's point of view," as I would like to have it understood in this context, carries a distribution of emphases that differs from the usual one: apart from the stress on the general mathematical techniques, the logical and the statistical aspects will be in the foreground. Furthermore, logics and statistics should be primarily, although not exclusively, viewed as the basic tools of "information theory." Also, that body of experience which has grown up around the planning, evaluating, and coding of complicated logical and mathematical automata will be the focus of much of this information theory. The most typical, but not the only, such automata are, of course, the large electronic computing machines.

Let me note, in passing, that it would be very satisfactory if one could talk about a "theory" of such automata. Regrettably, what at this moment exists—and to what I must appeal—can as yet be described only as an imperfectly articulated and hardly formalized "body of experience."

Lastly, my main aim is actually to bring out a rather different aspect of the matter. I suspect that a deeper mathematical study of the nervous system—"mathematical" in the sense outlined above—will affect our understanding of the aspects of mathematics itself that are involved. In fact, it may alter the way in which we look on mathematics and logics proper. I will try to explain my reasons for this belief later.

I begin by discussing some of the principles underlying the systematics and the practice of computing machines.

Existing computing machines fall into two broad classes: "analog" and "digital." This subdivision arises according to the way in which the numbers, on which the machine operates, are represented in it.

The Analog Procedure

In an analog machine each number is represented by a suitable physical quantity, whose values, measured in some pre-assigned unit, is equal to the number in question. This quantity may be the angle by which a certain disk has rotated, or the strength of a certain current, or the amount of a certain (relative) voltage, etc. To enable the machine to compute, i.e. to operate on these numbers according to a predetermined plan, it is necessary to provide organs (or components) that can perform on these representative quantities the basic operations of mathematics.

The Conventional Basic Operations

These basic operations are usually understood to be the "four species of arithmetic": addition (the operation $x + y$), subtraction $(x - y)$, multiplication (xy), division (x/y).

Thus it is obviously not difficult to add or to subtract two currents (by merging them in parallel or in antiparallel directions). Multiplication (of two currents) is more difficult, but there exist various kinds of electrical componentry which will perform this operation. The same is true for division (of one current by another). (For multiplication as well as for division —but not for addition and subtraction—of course the unit in which the current is measured is relevant.)

Unusual Basic Operations

A rather remarkable attribute of some analog machines, on which I will have to comment a good deal further, is this. Occasionally the machine is built around other "basic" operations than the four species of arithmetic mentioned above. Thus the classical "differential analyzer," which expresses numbers by the angles by which certain disks have rotated, proceeds as follows. Instead of addition, $x + y$, and subtraction, $x - y$, the operations $(x \pm y)/2$ are offered, because a readily available, simple component, the "differential gear" (the same one that is used on the back axle of an automobile) produces these. Instead of multiplication, xy, an entirely different procedure is used: In the differential analyzer all quantities appear as functions of time, and the differential analyzer makes use of an organ called the "integrator," which will, for two such quantities $x(t)$, $y(t)$ form the ("Stieltjes") integral $z(t) \equiv \int^t x(t)\, dy(t)$.

The point in this scheme is threefold:

First: the three above operations will, in suitable combinations, reproduce three of the four usual basic operations, namely addition, subtraction, and multiplication.

Second: in combination with certain "feedback" tricks, they will also generate the fourth operation, division. I will not discuss the feedback principle here, except by saying that while it has the appearance of a device for solving implicit relations, it is in reality a particularly elegant short-circuited iteration and successive approximation scheme.

Third, and this is the true justification of the differential analyzer: its basic operations $(x \pm y)/2$ and integration are, for wide classes of problems, more economical than the arithmetical ones $(x+y, x-y, xy, x/y)$. More specifically: any computing machine that is to solve a complex mathematical problem must be "programmed" for this task. This means that the complex operation of solving that problem must be replaced by a combination of the basic operations of the machine. Frequently it means something even more subtle: approximation of that operation—to any desired (prescribed) degree—by such combinations. Now for a given class of problems one set of basic operations may be more efficient, i.e. allow the use of simpler, less extensive, combinations, than another such set. Thus, in particular, for systems of total differential equations—for which the differential analyzer was primarily designed—the above-mentioned basic operations of that machine are more efficient than the previously mentioned arithmetical basic operations $(x + y, x - y, xy, x/y)$.

Next, I pass to the digital class of machines.

The Digital Procedure

In a decimal digital machine each number is represented in the same way as in conventional writing or printing, i.e. as a sequence of decimal digits. Each decimal digit, in turn, is represented by a system of "markers."

Markers, Their Combinations and Embodiments

A marker which can appear in ten different forms suffices by itself to represent a decimal digit. A marker which can appear in two different forms only will have to be used so that each decimal digit corresponds to a whole group. (A group of three two-valued markers allows 8 combinations; this is inadequate. A group of four such markers allows 16 combinations; this is more than adequate. Hence, groups of at least four markers must be used per decimal digit. There may be reasons to use larger groups; see below.) An example of a ten-valued marker is an electrical pulse that appears on one of ten pre-assigned lines. A two-valued marker is an electrical pulse on a pre-assigned line, so that its presence or absence conveys the information (the marker's "value"). Another possible two-valued marker is an electrical pulse that can have positive or negative polarity. There are, of course, many other equally valid marker schemes.

I will make one more observation on markers: The above-mentioned ten-valued marker is clearly a group of ten two-valued markers, in other words, highly redundant in the sense noted above. The minimum group, consisting of four two-valued markers, can also be introduced within the same framework. Consider a system of four pre-assigned lines, such that (simultaneous) electrical pulses can appear on any combination of these. This allows for 16 combinations, any 10 of which can be stipulated to correspond to the decimal digits.

Note that these markers, which are usually electrical pulses (or possibly electrical voltages or currents, lasting as long as their indication is to be valid), must be controlled by electrical gating devices.

Digital Machine Types and Their Basic Components

In the course of the development up to now, electrome-chanical relays, vacuum tubes, crystal diodes, ferromagnetic cores, and transistors have been successively used—some of them in combination with others, some of them preferably in the memory organs of the machine (cf. below), and others preferably outside the memory (in the "active" organs)—giving rise to as many different species of digital machines.

Parallel and Serial Schemes

Now a number in the machine is represented by a sequence of ten-valued markers (or marker groups), which may be arranged to appear simultaneously, in different organs of the machine—in *parallel*—or in temporal succession, in a single organ of the machine—in *series*. If the machine is built to handle, say, twelve-place decimal numbers, e.g. with six places "to the left" of the decimal point, and six "to the right," then twelve such markers (or marker groups) will have to be provided in each information channel of the machine that is meant for passing numbers. (This scheme can—and is in various machines—be made more flexible in various ways and degrees. Thus, in almost all machines, the position of the decimal point is adjustable. However, I will not go into these matters here any further.)

The Conventional Basic Operations

The operations of a digital machine have so far always been based on the four species of arithmetic. Regarding the well-known procedures that are being used, the following should be said:

First, on addition: in contrast to the physical processes that mediate this process in analog machines (cf. above), in this case rules of strict and logical character control this operation—how to form digital sums, when to produce a carry, and how to repeat and combine these operations. The logical nature of the digital sum becomes even clearer when the binary (rather than decimal) system is used. Indeed, the binary addition table (0 + 0 = 00, 0 + 1 = 1 + 0 = 01, 1 + 1 = 10) can be stated thus: The sum digit is 1 if the two addend digits differ, otherwise it is 0; the carry digit is 1 if both addend digits are 1, otherwise it is 0. Because of the possible presence of a carry digit, one actually needs a binary addition table for three terms (0 + 0 + 0 = 00, 0 + 0 + 1 = 0 + 1 + 0 = 1 + 0 + 0 = 01, 0 + 1 + 1 = 1 + 0 + 1 = 1 + 1 + 0 = 10, 1 + 1 + 1 = 11), and this states: The sum digit is 1, if the number of 1's among the addend (including the carry) digits is odd (1 or 3), otherwise it is 0; the carry digit is 1 if the 1's among the addend (including the carry) digits form a majority (2 or 3), otherwise it is 0.

Second, on subtraction: the logical structure of this is very similar to that one of addition. It can even be—and usually is—reduced to the latter by the simple device of "complementing" the subtrahend.

Third, on multiplication: the primarily logical character is even more obvious—and the structure more involved—than for addition. The products (of the multiplicand) with each digit of the multiplier are formed (usually preformed for all possible decimal digits, by various addition schemes), and then added together (with suitable shifts). Again, in the binary system the logical character is even more transparent and obvious. Since the only possible digits are 0 and 1, a (multiplier) digital product (of the multiplicand) is omitted for 0 and it is the multiplicand itself for 1.

All of this applies to products of positive factors. When both factors may have both signs, additional logical rules control the four situations that can arise.

Fourth, on division: the logical structure is comparable to that of the multiplication, except that now various iterated, trial-and-error subtraction procedures intervene, with specific logical rules (for the forming of the quotient digits) in the various alternative situations that can arise, and that must be dealt with according to a serial, repetitive scheme.

To sum up: all these operations now differ radically from the physical processes used in analog machines. They all are patterns of alternative actions, organized in highly repetitive sequences, and governed by strict and logical rules. Especially in the cases of multiplication and division these rules have a quite complex logical character. (This may be obscured by our long and almost instinctive familiarity with them, but if one forces oneself to state them fully, the degree of their complexity becomes apparent.)

Logical Control

Beyond the capability to execute the basic operations singly, a computing machine must be able to perform them according to the sequence—or rather, the logical pattern—in which they generate the solution of the mathematical problem that is the actual purpose of the calculation in hand. In the traditional analog machines—typified by the "differential analyzer"—this "sequencing" of the operation is achieved in this way. There must be a priori enough organs present in the machine to perform as many basic operations as the desired calculation calls for—i.e. enough "differential gears" and "integrators" (for the two basic operations $(x \pm y) / 2$ and $\int^t x(t) \, dy(t)$, respectively, cf. above). These—i.e. their "input" and "output" disks (or, rather, the axes of these)—must then be so connected to each other (by cogwheel connections in the early models, and by electrical follower-arrangements ["selsyns"] in the later ones) as to constitute a replica of the desired calculation. It should be noted that this connection-pattern can be set up at will—indeed, this is the means by which the problem to be solved, i.e. the intention of the user, is impressed on the machine. This "setting up" occurred in the early (cog wheel-connected, cf. above) machines by mechanical means, while in the later (electrically connected, cf. above) machines it was done by plugging. Nevertheless, it was in all these types always a fixed setting for the entire duration of a problem.

Plugged Control

In some of the very last analog machines a further trick was introduced. These had electrical, "plugged" connections. These plugged connections were actually controlled by electromechanical relays, and hence they could be changed by electrical stimulation of the magnets that closed or opened these relays. These electrical stimuli could be controlled by punched paper tapes, and these tapes could be started and stopped (and restarted and restopped, etc.) by electrical signals derived at suitable moments from the calculation.

Logical Tape Control

The latter reference means that certain numerical organs in the machine have reached certain preassigned conditions, e.g. that the sign of a certain number has turned negative, or that a certain number has been exceeded by another certain number, etc. Note that if numbers are defined by electrical voltages or currents, then their signs can be sensed by rectifier arrangements; for a rotating disk the sign shows whether it has passed a zero position moving right or moving left; a number is exceeded by another one when the sign of their difference turns negative, etc. Thus a "logical" tape control—or, better still, a "state of calculation combined with tape" control—was superposed over the basic, "fixed connections" control.

The digital machines started off-hand with different control systems. However, before discussing these I will make some general remarks that bear on digital machines, and on their relationship to analog machines.

The Principle of Only One Organ for Each Basic Operation

It must be emphasized, to begin with, that in digital machines there is uniformly only one organ for each basic operation. This contrasts with most analog machines, where there must be enough organs for each basic operation, depending on the requirements of the problem in hand (cf. above). It should be noted, however, that this is a historical fact rather than an intrinsic requirement—analog machines (of the electrically connected type, cf. above) could, in principle, be built with only one organ for each basic operation, and a logical control of any of the digital types to be described below. (Indeed, the reader can verify for himself without much difficulty, that the "very latest" type of analog machine control, described above, represents a transition to this modus operandi.)

It should be noted, furthermore, that some digital machines deviate more or less from this "only one organ for each basic operation" principle—but these deviations can be brought back to the orthodox scheme by rather simple reinterpretations. (In some cases it is merely a matter of dealing with a duplex [or multiplex] machine, with suitable means of intercommunication.) I will not go into these matters here any further.

The Consequent Need for a Special Memory Organ

The "only one organ for each basic operation" principle necessitates, however, the providing for a larger number of organs that can be used to store numbers passively—the results of various partial, intermediate calculations. That is, each such organ must be able to "store" a number—removing the one it may have stored previously—accepting it from some other organ to which it is at the time connected, and to "repeat" it upon "questioning": to emit it to some other organ to which it is at that (other) time connected. Such an organ is called a "memory register," the totality of these organs is called a "memory," and the number of registers in a memory in the "capacity" of that memory.

I can now pass to the discussion of the main modes of control for digital machines. This is best done by describing two basic types, and mentioning some obvious principles for combining them.

Control by "Control Sequence" Points

The first basic method of control, which has been widely used, can be described (with some simplifications and idealizations) as follows:

The machine contains a number of logical control organs, called "control sequence points," with the following function. (The number of these control sequence points can be quite considerable. In some newer machines it reaches several hundred.)

In the simplest mode of using this system, each control sequence point is connected to one of the basic operation organs that it actuates, and also to the memory registers which are to furnish the numerical inputs of this operation, and to the one that is to receive its output. After a definite delay (which must be sufficient for the performing of the operation), or after the receipt of a "performed" signal (if the duration of the operation is variable and its maximum indefinite or unacceptably long—this procedure requires, of course, an additional connection with the basic operation organ in question), the control sequence point actuates the next control sequence point, its "successor." This functions in turn, in a similar way, according to its own connections, etc. If nothing further is done, this furnishes the pattern for an unconditioned, repetitionless calculation.

More sophisticated patterns obtain if some control sequence points, to be called "branching points," are connected to two "successors" and are capable of two states, say A and B, so that A causes the process to continue by way of the first "successor" and B by way of the second one. The control sequence point is normally in state A, but it is connected to two memory registers, certain events in which

will cause it to go from A to B or from B to A, respectively—
say the appearance of a negative sign in the first one will
make it go from A to B, and the appearance of a negative
sign in the second one will make it go from B to A. (Note: in
addition to storing the digits of a number, cf. above, a memory register usually also stores its sign [+ or −]—for this
a two-valued marker suffices.) Now all sorts of possibilities
open up: The two "successors" may represent two altogether disjunct branches of the calculation, depending on
suitably assigned numerical criteria (controlling "A to B,"
while "B to A" is used to restore the original condition for a
new computation). Possibly the two alternative branches
may reunite later, in a common later successor. Still another
possibility arises when one of the two branches, say the one
controlled by A, actually leads back to the first mentioned
(branching) control sequence point. In this case one deals
with a repetitive procedure, which is iterated until a certain
numerical criterion is met (the one that commands "A to
B," cf. above). This is, of course, the basic iterative process.
All these tricks can be combined and superposed, etc.

Note that in this case, as in the plugged type control for
analog machines mentioned earlier, the totality of the (electrical) connections referred to constitutes the set-up of the
problem—the expression of the problem to be solved, i.e.
of the intention of the user. So this is again a plugged control. As in the case referred to, the plugged pattern can be

changed from one problem to another, but—at least in the simplest arrangement—it is fixed for the entire duration of a problem.

This method can be refined in many ways. Each control sequence point may be connected to several organs, stimulating more than one operation. The plugged connection may (as in an earlier example dealing with analog machines) actually be controlled by electromechanical relays, and these can be (as outlined there) set up by tapes, which in turn may move under the control of electrical signals derived from events in the calculation. I will not go here any further into all the variations that this theme allows.

Memory-Stored Control

The second basic method of control, which has actually gone quite far toward displacing the first one, can be described (again with some simplifications) as follows.

This scheme has, formally, some similarity with the plugged control scheme described above. However, the control sequence points are now replaced by "orders." An order is, in most embodiments of this scheme, physically the same thing as a number (of the kind with which the machine deals, cf. above). Thus in a decimal machine it is a sequence of decimal digits. (12 decimal digits in the example given previously, with or without making use of the sign, etc., cf. above. Sometimes more than one order is contained in this standard number space, but there is no need to go into this here.)

An order must indicate which basic operation is to be performed, from which memory registers the inputs of that operation are to come, and to which memory register its output is to go. Note that this presupposes that all memory registers are numbered serially—the number of a memory register is called its "address." It is convenient to number the basic operations, too. Then an order simply contains the number of its operation and the addresses of the memory registers referred to above, as a sequence of decimal digits (in a fixed order).

There are some variants on this, which, however, are not particularly important in the present context: An order may, in the way described above, control more than one operation; it may direct that the addresses that it contained be modified in certain specified ways before being applied in the process of its execution (the normally used—and practically most important—address modification consists of adding to all the addresses in question the contents of a specified memory register). Alternatively, these functions may be controlled by special orders, or an order may affect only part of any of the constituent actions described above.

A more important phase of each order is this. Like a control sequence point in the previous example, each order must determine its successor—with or without branching (cf. above). As I pointed out above, an order is usually "physically" the same thing as a number. Hence the natural way to store it—in the course of the problem in whose control it participates—is in a memory register. In other words, each order is stored in the memory, in a definite memory register, that is to say, at a definite address. This opens up a number of specific ways to handle the matter of an orders successor. Thus it may be specified that the successor of an order at the address X is—unless the opposite is made explicit—the order at the address $X + 1$. "The opposite" is a "transfer," a special order that specifies that the successor is at an assigned address Y. Alternatively, each order may have the "transfer" clause in it, i.e. specify explicitly the address of its successor. "Branching" is most conveniently handled by a "conditional transfer" order, which is one that specifies that the successor's address is X or Y, depending on whether a certain numerical condition has arisen or not—e.g. whether a number at a given address Z is negative or not. Such an order must then contain a number that characterizes this particular type of order (thus playing a similar role, and occupying the same position, as the basic operation number referred to further above), and the addresses X, Y, Z, as a sequence of decimal digits (cf. above).

Note the important difference between this mode of control and the plugged one, described earlier: There the control sequence points were real, physical objects, and their plugged connections expressed the problem. Now the orders are ideal entities, stored in the memory, and it is thus the contents of this particular segment of the memory that express the problem. Accordingly, this mode of control is called "memory-stored control."

Modus Operandi of the Memory-Stored Control

In this case, since the orders that exercise the entire control are in the memory, a higher degree of flexibility is achieved than in any previous mode of control. Indeed, the machine, under the control of its orders, can extract numbers (or orders) from the memory, process them (as numbers!), and return them to the memory (to the same or to other locations); i.e. it can change the contents of the memory—indeed this is its normal *modus operandi*. Hence it can, in particular, change the orders (since these are in the memory!)—the very orders that control its actions. Thus all sorts of sophisticated order-systems become possible, which keep successively modifying themselves and hence also the computational processes that are likewise under their control. In this way more complex processes than mere iterations become possible. Although all of this may sound far-fetched and complicated, such methods are widely used and very important in recent machine-computing—or, rather, computation-planning—practice.

Of course, the order-system—this means the problem to be solved, the intention of the user—is communicated to the machine by "loading" it into the memory. This is usually done from a previously prepared tape or some other similar medium.

Mixed Forms of Control

The two modes of control described in the above—the plugged and the memory-stored—allow various combinations, about which a few words may be said.

Consider a plugged control machine. Assume that it possesses a memory of the type discussed in connection with the memory-stored control machines. It is possible to describe the complete state of its plugging by a sequence of digits (of suitable length). This sequence can be stored in the memory; it is likely to occupy the space of several numbers, i.e. several, say consecutive, memory registers—in other words it will be found in a number of consecutive addresses, of which the first one may be termed its address, for short. The memory may be loaded with several such sequences, representing several different plugging schemes.

In addition to this, the machine may also have a complete control of the memory-stored type. Aside from the orders that go naturally with that system (cf. above), it should also have orders of the following types. First: an order that causes the plugged set-up to be reset according to the digital sequence stored at a specified memory address (cf. above). Second: a system of orders which change specified single items of plugging. (Note that both of these provisions necessitate that the plugging be actually effected by electrically controllable devices, i.e. by electromechanical relays [cf. the earlier discussion] or by vacuum tubes or by ferromagnetic cores, or the like.) Third: an order which turns the control of the machine from the memory-stored regime to the plugged regime.

It is, of course, also necessary that the plugging scheme be able to designate the memory-stored control (presumably at a specified address) as the successor (or, in case of branching, as one successor) of a control sequence point.

Mixed Numerical Procedures

These remarks should suffice to give a picture of the flexibility which is inherent in these control modes and their combinations.

A further class of "mixed" machine types that deserve mention is that where the analog and the digital principles occur together. To be more exact: This is a scheme where part of the machine is analog, part is digital, and the two communicate with each other (for numerical material) and are subject to a common control. Alternatively, each part may have its own control, in which case these two controls must communicate with each other (for logical material). This arrangement requires, of course, organs that can convert a digitally given number into an analogically given one, and conversely. The former means building up a continuous quantity from its digital expression, the latter means measuring a continuous quantity and expressing the result in digital form. Components of various kinds that perform these two tasks are well known, including fast electrical ones.

Mixed Representations of Numbers. Machines Built on This Basis

Another significant class of "mixed" machine types comprises those machines in which each step of the computing procedure (but, of course, not of the logical procedure) combines analog and digital principles. The simplest occurrence of this is when each number is represented in a part analog, part digital way. I will describe one such scheme, which has occasionally figured in component and machine construction and planning, and in certain types of communications, although no large-scale machine has ever been based on its use.

In this system, which I shall call the "pulse density" system, each number is expressed by a sequence of successive electrical pulses (on a single line), so that the length of this sequence is indifferent but the average density of the pulse sequence (in time) is the number to be represented. Of course, one must specify two time intervals t_1, t_2 (t_2 being considerably larger than t_1), so that the averaging in question must be applied to durations lying between t_1 and t_2. The unit of the number in question, when equated to this density, must be specified. Occasionally, it is convenient to let the density in question be equal not to the number itself but to a suitable (fixed) monotone function of it—e.g. the logarithm. (The purpose of this latter device is to obtain a better resolution of this representation when it is needed—when the number is small—and a poorer one when it is acceptable—when the number is large—and to have all continuous shadings of this.)

It is possible to devise organs which apply the four species of arithmetic to these numbers. Thus when the densities represent the numbers themselves, addition can be effected by combining the two sequences. The other operations are somewhat trickier—but adequate, and more or less elegant, procedures exist there, too. I shall not discuss how negative numbers, if needed, are represented—this is easily handled by suitable tricks, too.

In order to have adequate precision, every sequence must contain many pulses within each time interval t_1 mentioned above. If, in the course of the calculation, a number is desired to change, the density of its sequence can be made to change accordingly, provided that this process is slow compared to the time interval t_2 mentioned above.

For this type of machine the sensing of numerical conditions (e.g. for logical control purposes, cf. above) may be quite tricky. However, there are various devices which will convert such a number, i.e. a density of pulses in time, into an analog quantity. (E.g. the density of pulses, each of which delivers a standard charge to a slowly leaking condenser [through a given resistance] will control it to a reasonably constant voltage level and leakage current—both of which are usable analog quantities.) These analog quantities can then be used for logical control, as discussed previously.

After this description of the general principles of the functioning and control of computing machines, I will go on to some remarks about their actual use and the principles that govern it.

Precision

Let me, first, compare the use of analog machines and of digital machines.

Apart from all other considerations, the main limitation of analog machines relates to precision. Indeed, the precision of electrical analog machines rarely exceeds $1:10^3$, and even mechanical ones (like the differential analyzer) achieve at best $1:10^4$ to 10^5. Digital machines, on the other hand, can achieve any desired precision; e.g. the twelve-decimal machine referred to earlier (for the reasons to be discussed further below, this is a rather typical level of precision for a modern digital machine) represents, of course, a precision $1:10^{12}$. Note also that increasing precision is much easier in a digital than in an analog regime: To go from $1:10^3$ to $1:10^4$ in a differential analyzer is relatively simple; from $1:10^4$ to $1:10^5$ is about the best present technology can do; from $1:10^5$ to

$1:10^6$ is (with present means) impossible. On the other hand, to go from $1:10^{12}$ to $1:10^{13}$ in a digital machine means merely adding one place to twelve; this means usually no more than a relative increase in equipment (not every-where!) of $1/12 = 8.3$ per cent, and an equal loss in speed (not everywhere!)—none of which is serious. The pulse density system is comparable to the analog system; in fact it is worse: the precision is intrinsically low. Indeed, a precision of $1:10^2$ requires that there be usually 10^2 pulses in the time interval t_1 (cf. above)—i.e. the speed of the machine is reduced by this fact alone by a factor of 100. Losses in speed of this order are, as a rule, not easy to take, and significantly larger ones would usually be considered prohibitive.

Reasons for the High (Digital) Precision Requirements

However, at this point another question arises: why are such extreme precisions (like the digital $1:10^{12}$) at all necessary? Why are the typical analog precisions (say $1:10^4$), or even those of the pulse density system (say $1:10^2$), not adequate? In most problems of applied mathematics and engineering the data are no better than $1:10^3$ or $1:10^4$, and often they do not even reach the level of $1:10^2$, and the answers are not required or meaningful with higher precisions either. In chemistry, biology, or economics, or in other practical matters, the precision levels are usually even less exacting. It has nevertheless been the uniform experience in modern high speed computing that even precision levels like $1:10^5$ are inadequate for a large part of important problems, and that digital machines with precision levels like $1:10^{10}$ and $1:10^{12}$ are fully justified in practice. The reasons for this surprising phenomenon are interesting and significant. They are connected with the inherent structure of our present mathematical and numerical procedures.

The characteristic fact regarding these procedures is that when they are broken down into their constituent elements, they turn out to be very long. This holds for all problems that justify the use of a fast computing machine—i.e. for all that have at least a medium degree of complexity. The underlying reason is that our present computational methods call for analyzing all mathematical functions into combinations of basic operations—and this means usually the four species of arithmetic, or something fairly comparable. Actually, most functions can only be approximated in this way, and this means in most cases quite long, possibly iteratively defined, sequences of basic operations (cf. above). In other words, the "arithmetical depth" of the necessary operations is usually quite great. Note that the "logical depth" is still greater, and by a considerable factor—that is, if, e.g., the four species of arithmetic are broken down into the underlying logical steps (cf. above), each one of them is a long logical chain by itself. However, I need to consider here only the arithmetical depth.

Now if there are large numbers of arithmetical operations, the errors occurring in each operation are superposed. Since they are in the main (although not entirely) random, it follows that if there are N operations, the error will not be increased N times, but about $\sqrt{N}$ times. This by itself will not, as a rule, suffice to necessitate a stepwise $1:10^{12}$ precision for an over-all $1:10^3$ result (cf. above). For this to be so, $1/10^{12}\sqrt{N} \sim 1/10^3$ would be needed, i.e. $N \sim 10^{16}$, whereas even in the fastest modern machines N gets hardly larger than 10^{10}. (A machine that performs an arithmetical operation every 20 microseconds, and works on a single problem 48 hours, represents a rather extreme case. Yet even here only $N \sim 10^{10}$!) However, another circumstance supervenes. The operations performed in the course of the calculation may amplify errors that were introduced by earlier operations. This can cover any numerical gulf very quickly. The ratio used above, $1:10^3$ to $1:10^{12}$, is 10^9, yet 425 successive operations each of which increases an error by 5 per cent only, will account for it! I will not attempt any detailed and realistic estimate here, particularly because the art of computing consists to no small degree of measures to keep this effect down. The conclusion from a great deal of experience has been, at any rate, that the high precision levels referred to above are justified, as soon as reasonably complicated problems are met with.

Before leaving the immediate subject of computing machines, I will say a few things about their speeds, sizes, and the like.

Characteristics of Modern Analog Machines

The order of magnitude of the number of basic-operations organs in the largest existing analog machines is one or two hundred. The nature of these organs depends, of course, on the analog process used. In the recent past they have tended uniformly to be electrical or at least electromechanical (the mechanical stage serving for enhanced precision, cf. above). Where an elaborate logical control is provided (cf. above), this adds to the system (like all logical control of this type) certain typical digital action organs, like electromechanical relays or vacuum tubes (the latter would, in this case, not be driven at extreme speeds). The numbers of these may go as high as a few thousands. The investment represented by such a machine may, in extreme cases, reach the order of $1,000,000.

Characteristics of Modern Digital Machines

The organization of large digital machines is more complex. They are made up of "active" organs and of organs serving "memory" functions—I will include among the latter the "input" and "output" organs, although this is not common practice.

The active organs are the following. First, organs which perform the basic logical actions: sense coincidences, combine stimuli, and possibly sense anticoincidences (no more than this is necessary, although sometimes organs for more complex logical operations are also provided). Second, organs which regenerate pulses: restore their gradually attrited energy, or simply lift them from the energy level prevailing in one part of the machine to another (higher) energy level prevailing in another part (these two functions are called amplification)—which restore the desired (i.e. within certain tolerances, standardized) pulse-shape and timing. Note that the first-mentioned logical operations are the elements from which the arithmetical ones are built up (cf. above).

Active Components; Questions of Speed

All these functions have been performed, in historical succession, by electromechanical relays, vacuum tubes, crystal diodes, and ferromagnetic cores and transistors (cf. above), or by various small circuits involving these. The relays permitted achieving speeds of about 10^{-2} seconds per elementary logical action, the vacuum tubes permitted improving this to the order of 10^{-5} to 10^{-6} seconds (in extreme cases even one-half or one-quarter of the latter). The last group, collectively known as solid-state devices, came in on the 10^{-6} second (in some cases a small multiple of this) level, and is likely to extend the speed range to 10^{-7} seconds per elementary logical action, or better. Other devices, which I will not discuss here, are likely to carry us still farther—I expect that before another decade passes we will have reached the level of 10^{-8} to 10^{-9} seconds.

Number of Active Components Required

The number of active organs in a large modern machine varies, according to type, from, say, 3,000 to, say, 30,000. Within this, the basic (arithmetical) operations are usually performed by one subassembly (or, rather, by one, more or less merged, group of subassemblies), the "arithmetical organ." In a large modern machine this organ consists, according to type, of approximately 300 to 2,000 active organs.

As will appear further below, certain aggregates of active organs are used to perform some memory functions. These comprise, typically, 200 to 2,000 active organs.

Finally the (properly) "memory" aggregates (cf. below) require ancillary subassemblies of active organs, to service and administer them. For the fastest memory group that does not consist of active organs (cf. below; in the terminology used there, this is the second level of the memory hierarchy), this function may require about 300 to 2,000 active organs. For all parts of the memory together, the corresponding requirements of ancillary active organs may amount to as much as 50 per cent of the entire machine.

Memory Organs. Access Times and Memory Capacities

The memory organs belong to several different classes. The characteristic by which they are classified is the "access time." The access time is defined as follows. First: the time required to store a number which is already present in some other part of the machine (usually in a register of active organs, cf. below)—removing the number that the memory organ may have been storing before. Second: the time required to "repeat" the number stored—upon "questioning"—to another part of the machine, which can accept it (usually to a register of active organs, cf. below). It may be convenient to distinguish between these two access times ("in" and "out"), or to use a single one, the larger of the two, or, possibly, their average. Also, the access time may or may not vary from occasion to occasion—if it does not depend on the memory address, it is called "random access." Even if it is variable, a single value may be used, the maximum, or possibly the average, access time. (The latter may, of course, depend on the statistical properties of the problems to be solved.) At any rate, I will use here, for the sake of simplicity, a single access time.

Memory Registers Built from Active Organs

Memory registers can be built out of active organs (cf. above). These have the shortest access time, and are the most expensive. Such a register is, together with its access facilities, a circuit of at least four vacuum tubes (or, alternatively, not significantly fewer solid state devices) per binary digit (or for a sign), hence, at least four times the number per decimal digit (cf. above). Thus the twelve-decimal digit (and sign) number system, referred to earlier, would normally require in these terms a 196-tube register. On the other hand, such registers have access times of one or two elementary reaction times—which is very fast when compared to other possibilities (cf. below). Also, several registers of this type can be integrated with certain economies in equipment; they are needed in any case as "in" and "out" access organs for other types of memories; one or two (in some designs even three) of them are needed as parts of the arithmetic organ. To sum up: in moderate numbers they are more economical than one might at first expect, and they are, to that extent, also necessary as subordinate parts of other organs of the machine. However, they do not seem to be suited to furnish the large capacity memories that are needed in nearly all large computing machines. (This last observation applies only to modern machines, i.e. those of the vacuum-tube epoch and after. Before that, in relay machines—cf. above—relays were used as active organs, and relay registers were used as the main form of memory. Hence the discussion that follows, too, is to be understood as referring to modern machines only.)

The Hierarchic Principle for Memory Organs

For these extensive memory capacities, then, other types of memory must be used. At this point the "hierarchy" principle of memory intervenes. The significance of this principle is the following:

For its proper functioning—to solve the problems for which it is intended—a machine may need a capacity of a certain number, say N words, at a certain access time, say t. Now it may be technologically difficult, or—which is the way in which such difficulties usually manifest themselves—very expensive, to provide N words with access time t. However, it may not be necessary to have all the N words at this access time. It may well be that a considerably smaller number, say N', is needed at the access time t. Furthermore, it may be that—once N' words at access time t are provided—the entire capacity of N words is only needed at a longer access time t''. Continuing in this direction, it may further happen that it is most economical to provide certain intermediate capacities in addition to the above—capacities of fewer than N but more than N' words, at access times which are longer than t but shorter than t''. The most general scheme in this regard is to provide a sequence of capacities $N_1, N_2, \ldots, N_{k-1}, N_k$ and of access times $t_1, t_2, \ldots, t_{k-1}, t_k$, so that these capacities get more exacting and the access times less exacting as a sequence progresses—i.e. $N_1 < N_2 < \cdots < N_{k+1} < N_k$ and $t_1 < t_2 < \cdots < t_{k-1} < t_k$—so that N_i words are

34

required at access time t_i for each $i = 1, 2, \cdots, k - 1, k$. (In order to adjust this to what was said previously, one must assume that $N_1 = N'$, $t_1 = t$, and $N_k = N$, $t_k = t''$.) In this scheme, each value of i represents one level in the hierarchy of memories, and the hierarchy has k such levels.

Memory Components; Questions of Access

In a large-scale, modern, high-speed computing machine, a complete count of all levels of the memory hierarchy will disclose at least three and possibly four or five such levels.

The first level always corresponds to the registers mentioned above. Their number, N_1, is in almost any machine design at least three and sometimes higher—numbers as high as twenty have occasionally been proposed. The access time, t_1, is the basic switching time of the machine (or possibly twice that time).

The next (second) level in the hierarchy is always achieved with the help of specific memory organs. These are different from the switching organs used in the rest of the machine (and in the first level of the hierarchy, cf. above). The memory organs now in use for this level usually have memory capacities, N_2, ranging from a few thousand words to as much as a few tens of thousands (sizes of the latter kind are at present still in the design stage). The access time, t_2, is usually five to ten times longer than the one of the previous level, t_1. Further levels usually correspond to an increase in memory capacity, N_i, by some factor like 10 at each step. The access times, t_i, increase even faster, but here other limiting and qualifying rules regarding the access time also intervene (cf. below). A detailed discussion of this subject would call for a degree of detail that does not seem warranted at this time.

The fastest components, which are specifically memory organs (i.e. not active organs, cf. above), are certain electrostatic devices and magnetic core arrays. The use of the latter seems to be definitely on the ascendant, although other techniques (electrostatic, ferro-electric, etc.), may also re-enter or enter the picture. For the later levels of the memory hierarchy, magnetic drums and magnetic tapes are at present mostly in use; magnetic discs have been suggested and occasionally explored.

Complexities of the Concept of Access Time

The three last-mentioned devices are all subject to special access rules and limitations: a magnetic drum memory presents all its parts successively and cyclically for access; the memory capacity of a tape is practically unlimited, but it presents its parts in a fixed linear succession, which can be stopped and reversed when desired; all these schemes can be combined with various arrangements that provide for special synchronisms between the machine's functioning and the fixed memory sequences.

The very last stage of any memory hierarchy is necessarily the outside world—that is, the outside world as far as the machine is concerned, i.e. that part of it with which the machine can directly communicate, in other words the input and the output organs of the machine. These are usually punched paper tapes or cards, and on the output side, of course, also printed paper. Sometimes a magnetic tape is the ultimate input-output system of the machine, and its translation onto a medium that a human can directly use—i.e. punched or printed paper—is performed apart from the machine.

The following are some access times in absolute terms: For existing ferromagnetic core memories, 5 to 15 microseconds; for electrostatic memories, 8 to 20 microseconds; for magnetic drums, 2,500 to 20,000 rpm., i.e. a revolution per 24 to 3 milliseconds—in this time 1 to 2,000 words may get fed; for magnetic tapes, speeds up to 70,000 lines per second, i.e. a line in 14 microseconds; a word may consist of 5 to 15 lines.

The Principle of Direct Addressing

All existing machines and memories use "direct addressing," which is to say that every word in the memory has a numerical address of its own that characterizes it and its position within the memory (the total aggregate of all hierarchic levels) uniquely. This numerical address is always explicitly specified when the memory word is to be read or written. Sometimes not all parts of the memory are accessible at the same time (cf. above; there may also be multiple memories, not all of which can be acceded to at the same time, with certain provisions for access priorities). In this case, access to the memory depends on the general state of the machine at the moment when access is requested. Nevertheless, there is never any ambiguity about the address, and the place it designates.

The discussion up to this point has provided the basis for the comparison that is the objective of this work. I have described, in some detail, the nature of modern computing machines and the broad alternative principles around which they can be organized. It is now possible to pass on to the other term of the comparison, the human nervous system. I will discuss the points of similarity and dissimilarity between these two kinds of "automata." Bringing out the elements of similarity leads over well-known territory. There are elements of dissimilarity, too, not only in rather obvious respects of size and speed but also in certain much deeper-lying areas: These involve the principles of functioning and control, of over-all organization, etc. My primary aim is to develop some of these. However, in order to appreciate them properly, a juxtaposition and combination with the points of similarity, as well as with those of more superficial dissimilarity (size, speed; cf. above) are also required. Hence the discussion must place considerable emphasis on these, too.

Simplified Description of the
Function of the Neuron

The most immediate observation regarding the nervous system is that its functioning is *prima facie* digital. It is necessary to discuss this fact, and the structures and functions on which its assertion is based, somewhat more fully.

The basic component of this system is the *nerve cell*, the *neuron*, and the normal function of a neuron is to generate and to propagate a *nerve impulse*. This impulse is a rather complex process, which has a variety of aspects—electrical, chemical, and mechanical. It seems, nevertheless, to be a reasonably uniquely defined process, i.e. nearly the same under all conditions; it represents an essentially reproducible, unitary response to a rather wide variety of stimuli.

Let me discuss this—i.e. those aspects of the nerve impulse that seem to be the relevant ones in the present context—in somewhat more detail.

The Nature of the Nerve Impulse

The nerve cell consists of a *body* from which originate, directly or indirectly, one or more branches. Such a branch is called an *axon* of the cell. The nerve impulse is a continuous change, propagated—usually at a fixed speed, which may, however, be a function of the nerve cell involved—along the (or rather, along each) axon. As mentioned above, this condition can be viewed under multiple aspects. One of its characteristics is certainly that it is an electrical disturbance; in fact, it is most frequently described as being just that. This disturbance is usually an electrical potential of something like 50 millivolts and of about a millisecond's duration. Concurrently with this electrical disturbance there also occur chemical changes along the axon. Thus, in the area of the axon over which the pulse-potential is passing, the ionic constitution of the intracellular fluid changes, and so do the electrical-chemical properties (conductivity, permeability) of the wall of the axon, the membrane. At the endings of the axon the chemical character of the change is even more obvious; there, specific and characteristic substances make their appearance when the pulse arrives. Finally, there are probably mechanical changes as well. Indeed, it is very likely that the changes of the various ionic permeabilities of the cell membrane (cf. above) can come about only by reorientation of its molecules, i.e. by mechanical changes involving the relative positions of these constituents.

It should be added that all these changes are reversible. In other words, when the impulse has passed, all conditions along the axon, and all its constituent parts, resume their original states.

Since all these effects occur on a molecular scale—the thickness of the cell membrane is of the order of a few tenth-microns (i.e. 10^{-5} cm.), which is a molecular dimension for the large organic molecules that are involved here—the above distinctions between electrical, chemical, and mechanical effects are not so definite as it might first appear. Indeed, on the molecular scale there are no sharp distinctions between all these kinds of changes: every chemical change is induced by a change in intramolecular forces which determine changed relative positions of the molecules, i.e. it is mechanically induced. Furthermore, every such intramolecular mechanical change alters the electrical properties of the molecule involved, and therefore induces changed electrical properties and changed relative electrical potential levels. To sum up: on the usual (macroscopic) scale, electrical, chemical, and mechanical processes represent alternatives between which sharp distinctions can be maintained. However, on the near-molecule level of the nerve membrane, all these aspects tend to merge. It is, therefore, not surprising that the nerve impulse turns out to be a phenomenon which can be viewed under any one of them.

The Process of Stimulation

As I mentioned before, the fully developed nerve impulses are comparable, no matter how induced. Because their character is not an unambiguously defined one (it may be viewed electrically as well as chemically, cf. above), its induction, too, can be alternatively attributed to electrical or to chemical causes. Within the nervous system, however, it is mostly due to one or more other nerve impulses. Under such conditions, the process of its induction—the *stimulation* of a nerve impulse—may or may not succeed. If it fails, a passing disturbance arises at first, but after a few milliseconds, this dies out. Then no disturbances propagate along the axon. If it succeeds, the disturbance very soon assumes a (nearly) standard form, and in this form it spreads along the axon. That is to say, as mentioned above, a standard nerve impulse will then move along the axon, and its appearance will be reasonably independent of the details of the process that induced it.

The stimulation of the nerve impulse occurs normally in or near the body of the nerve cell. Its propagation, as discussed above, occurs along the axon.

The Mechanism of Stimulating Pulses by Pulses;
Its Digital Character

I can now return to the digital character of this mechanism. The nervous pulses can clearly be viewed as (two-valued) markers, in the sense discussed previously: the absence of a pulse then represents one value (say, the binary digit o), and the presence of one represents the other (say, the binary digit 1). This must, of course, be interpreted as an occurrence on a specific axon (or, rather, on all the axons of a specific neuron), and possibly in a specific time relation to other events. It is, then, to be interpreted as a marker (a binary digit o or 1) in a specific, logical role.

As mentioned above, pulses (which appear on the axons of a given neuron) are usually stimulated by other pulses that are impinging on the body of the neuron. This stimulation is, as a rule, conditional, i.e. only certain combinations and synchronisms of such primary pulses stimulate the secondary pulse in question—all others will fail to so stimulate. That is, the neuron is an organ which accepts and emits definite physical entities, the pulses. Upon receipt of pulses in certain combinations and synchronisms it will be stimulated to emit a pulse of its own, otherwise it will not emit. The rules which describe to which groups of pulses it will so respond are the rules that govern it as an active organ.

This is clearly the description of the functioning of an organ in a digital machine, and of the way in which the role and function of a digital organ has to be characterized. It therefore justifies the original assertion, that the nervous system has a *prima facie* digital character.

Let me add a few words regarding the qualifying "prima facie." The above description contains some idealizations and simplifications, which will be discussed subsequently. Once these are taken into account, the digital character no longer stands out quite so clearly and unequivocally. Nevertheless, the traits emphasized in the above are the primarily conspicuous ones. It seems proper, therefore, to begin the discussion as I did here, by stressing the digital character of the nervous system.

Time Characteristics of Nerve Response, Fatigue, and Recovery

Before going into this, however, some orienting remarks on the size, energy requirements, and speed of the nerve cell are in order. These will be particularly illuminating when stated in terms of comparisons with the main "artificial" competitors: The typical active organs of modern logical and computing machines. These are, of course, the vacuum tube and (more recently) the transistor.

I stated above that the stimulation of the nerve cell occurs normally on or near its body. Actually, a perfectly normal stimulation is possible along an axon, too. That is, an adequate electrical potential or a suitable chemical stimulant in adequate concentration, when applied at a point of the axon, will start there a disturbance which soon develops into a standard pulse, traveling both up and down the axon, from the point stimulated. Indeed, the "usual" stimulation described above mostly takes place on a set of branches extending from the body of the cell for a short distance, which, apart from their smaller dimensions, are essentially axons themselves, and it propagates from these to the body of the nerve cell (and then to the regular axons). By the way, these stimulation-receptors are called *dendrites*. The normal stimulation, when it comes from another pulse (or pulses) emanates from a special ending of the axon (or axons) that propagated the pulse in question. This ending is called a *synapse*. (Whether a pulse can stimulate only through a synapse, or whether, in traveling along an axon, it can stimulate directly another, exceptionally close-lying axon, is a question that need not be discussed here. The appearances are in favor of assuming that such a short-circuited process is possible.) The time of trans-synaptic stimulation amounts to a few times 10^{-4} seconds, this time being defined as the duration between the arrival of a pulse at a synapse and the appearance of the stimulated pulse on the nearest point of an axon of the stimulated neuron. However, this is not the most significant way to define the reaction time of a neuron, when viewed as an active organ in a logical machine. The reason for this is that immediately after the stimulated pulse has become evident, the stimulated neuron has not yet reverted to its original, prestimulation condition. It is *fatigued*, i.e. it could not immediately accept stimulation by another pulse and respond in the standard way. From the point of view of machine economy, it is a more important measure of speed to state after how much time a stimulation that induced a standard response can be followed by another stimulation that will also induce a standard response. This duration is about 1.5 times 10^{-2} seconds. It is clear from these figures that only one or two per cent of this time is needed for the actual trans-synaptic stimulation, the remainder representing recovery time, during which the neuron returns from its fatigued, immediate post-stimulation condition to its normal, prestimulation one. It should be noted that this recovery from fatigue is a gradual one—already at a certain earlier time (after about .5 times 10^{-2} seconds) the neuron can respond in a nonstandard way, namely it will produce a standard pulse, but only in response to a stimulus which is significantly stronger than the one needed under standard conditions. This circumstance has somewhat broad significance, and I will come back to it later on.

Thus the reaction time of a neuron is, depending on how one defines it, somewhere between 10^{-4} and 10^{-2} seconds, but the more significant definition is the latter one. Compared to this, modern vacuum tubes and transistors can be used in large logical machines at reaction times between 10^{-6} and 10^{-7} seconds. (Of course, I am allowing here, too, for the complete recovery time; the organ in question is, after this duration, back to its prestimulation condition.) That is, our artifacts are, in this regard, well ahead of the corresponding natural components, by factors like 10^4 to 10^5.

With respect to size, matters have a rather different aspect. There are various ways to evaluate size, and it is best to take these up one by one.

Size of a Neuron. Comparisons with Artificial Components

The linear size of a neuron varies widely from one nerve cell to the other, since some of these cells are contained in closely integrated large aggregates and have, therefore, very short axons, while others conduct pulses between rather remote parts of the body and may, therefore, have linear extensions comparable to those of the entire human body. One way to obtain an unambiguous and significant comparison is to compare the logically active part of the nerve cell with that of a vacuum tube, or transistor. For the former this is the cell membrane, whose thickness as mentioned before is of the order of a few times 10^{-5} cm. For the latter it is as follows: in the case of the vacuum tube, it is the grid-to-cathode distance, which varies from 10^{-1} to a few times 10^{-2} cm.; in the case of the transistor, it is the distance between the so-called "whisker electrodes" (the non-ohmic electrodes—the "emitter" and the "control-electrode"), about 3 folded in order to account for the immediate, active environment of these subcomponents, and this amounts to somewhat less than 10^{-2} cm. Thus, with regard to linear size, the natural components seem to lead our artifacts by a factor like 10^{3}.

Next, a comparison with respect to volume is possible. The central nervous system occupies a space of the order magnitude of a liter (in the brain), i.e. of 10^{3} cm.^{3} The number of neurons contained in this system is usually estimated to be of the order of 10^{10}, or somewhat higher. This would allow about 10^{-7} cm.^{3} per neuron.

The density with which vacuum tubes or transistors can be packed can also be estimated—although not with absolute unambiguity. It seems clear that this packing density is (on either side of the comparison) a better measure of size efficiency than the actual volume of a single component. With present-day techniques, aggregates of a few thousand vacuum tubes will certainly occupy several times 10 ft.^{3}; for transistors the same may be achieved, in something like one, or a few, ft.^{3} Using the figure of the latter order as a measure of the best that can be done today, one obtains something like 10^5 cm.^{3} for a few times 10^3 active organs, i.e. about 10 to 10^2 cm.^{3} per active organ. Thus the natural components lead the artificial ones with respect to volume requirements by factors like 10^8 to 10^9. In comparing this with the estimates for the linear size, it is probably best to consider the linear size-factor as being on one footing with the cube root of the volume-factor. The cube root of the above 10^8 to 10^9 is .5 to 1 times 10^3. This is in good accord with the 10^2 arrived at above by a direct method.

Energy Dissipation. Comparisons with Artificial Components

Finally, a comparison can be made with respect to energy consumption. As active logical organ does not, by its nature, do any work: the stimulated pulse that it produces need not have more energy than the prorated fraction of the pulses which stimulate it—and in any case there is no intrinsic and necessary relationship between these energies. Consequently, the energy involved is almost entirely dissipated, i.e. converted into heat without doing relevant mechanical work. Thus the energy consumed is actually energy dissipated, and one might as well talk about the energy dissipation of such organs.

The energy dissipation in the human central nervous system (in the brain) is of the order of 10 watts. Since, as pointed out above, the order of 10^{10} neurons are involved here, this means a dissipation of 10^{-9} watts per neuron. The typical dissipation of a vacuum tube is of the order of 5 to 10 watts. The typical dissipation of a transistor may be as little as 10^{-1} watts. Thus the natural components lead the artificial ones with respect to dissipation by factors like 10^8 to 10^9—the same factors that appeared above with respect to volume requirements.

Summary of Comparisons

Summing up all of this, it appears that the relevant comparison-factor with regard to size is about 10^8 to 10^9 in favor of the natural componentry versus the artificial one. This factor is obtained from the cube of a linear comparison, as well as by a volume-comparison and an energy-dissipation comparison. Against this there is a factor of about 10^4 to 10^5 on speed in favor of the artificial componentry versus the natural one.

On these quantitative evaluations certain conclusions can be based. It must be remembered, of course, that the discussion is still moving very near to the surface, so that conclusions arrived at at this stage are very much subject to revision in the light of the further progress of the discussion. It seems nevertheless worth while to formulate certain conclusions at this point. They are the following ones.

First: in terms of the number of actions that can be performed by active organs of the same total size (defined by volume or by energy dissipation) in the same interval, the natural componentry is a factor 10^4 ahead of the artificial one. This is the quotient of the two factors obtained above, i.e. of 10^8 to 10^9 by 10^4 to 10^5.

Second: the same factors show that the natural componentry favors automata with more, but slower, organs, while the artificial one favors the reverse arrangement of fewer, but faster, organs. Hence it is to be expected that an efficiently organized large natural automation (like the human nervous system) will tend to pick up as many logical (or informational) items as possible simultaneously, and process them simultaneously, while an efficiently organized large artificial automation (like a large modern computing machine) will be more likely to do things successively— one thing at a time, or at any rate not so many things at a time. That is, large and efficient natural automata are likely to be highly *parallel*, while large and efficient artificial automata will tend to be less so, and rather to be *serial*. (Cf. some earlier remarks on parallel versus serial arrangements.)

Third: it should be noted, however, that parallel and serial operation are not unrestrictedly substitutable for each other—as would be required to make the first remark above completely valid, with its simple scheme of dividing the size-advantage factor by the speed-disadvantage factor in order to get a single (efficiency) "figure of merit." More specifically, not everything serial can be immediately paralleled—certain operations can only be performed after certain others, and not simultaneously with them (i.e. they must use the results of the latter). In such a case, the transition from a serial scheme to a parallel one may be impossible, or it may be possible but only concurrently with a change in the logical approach and organization of the procedure. Conversely, the desire to serialize a parallel procedure may impose new requirements on the automaton. Specifically, it will almost always create new memory requirements, since the results of the operations that are performed first must be stored while the operations that come after these are performed. Hence the logical approach and structure in natural automata may be expected to differ widely from those in artificial automata. Also, it is likely that the memory requirements of the latter will turn out to be systematically more severe than those of the former.

All these viewpoints will reappear in the discussions that are to follow.

Stimulation Criteria

The Simplest—Elementary Logical

I can now turn to the discussion of the idealizations and simplifications contained in the description of nerve-action as it was given further above. I pointed out there that these existed and that their implications are not at all trivial to evaluate.

As pointed out before, the normal output of a neuron is the standard nerve pulse. This can be induced by various forms of stimulation, including the arrival of one or more pulses from other neurons. Other possible stimulators are phenomena in the outside world to which a particular neuron is specifically sensitive (light, sound, pressure, temperature), and physical and chemical changes within the organism at the point where the neuron is situated. I will begin by considering the first-mentioned form of stimulation—that by other nerve pulses.

I observed before that this particular mechanism—the stimulation of nerve pulses by suitable combinations of other nerve pulses—makes the neuron comparable to the typical basic, digital, active organ. To elaborate this further: if a neuron is contacted (by way of their synapses) by the axons of two other neurons, and if its minimum stimulation requirement (in order to evoke a response pulse) is that of two (simultaneous) incoming pulses, then this neuron is in fact an "and" organ: it performs the logical operation of conjunction (verbalized by "and"), since it responds only when both its stimulators are (simultaneously) active. If, on the other hand, the minimum requirement is merely the arrival (at least) of one pulse, the neuron is an "or" organ—i.e. it performs the logical operation of disjunction (verbalized by "or"), since it responds when either of its two stimulators is active.

"And" and "or" are the basic operations of logic. Together with "no" (the logical operation of negation) they are a complete set of basic logical operations—all other logical operations, no matter how complex, can be obtained by suitable combinations of these. I will not discuss here how neurons can simulate the operation "no" too, or by what tricks the use of this operation can be avoided altogether. The above should suffice to make clear what I have already emphasized earlier, that the neurons appear, when thus viewed, as the basic logical organs—and hence also as the basic digital organs.

More Complicated Stimulation Criteria

This, however, is a simplification and idealization of reality. The actual neurons are, as a rule, not so simply organized with respect to their position in the system.

Some neurons do indeed have only one or two—or at any rate a few, easily enumerated—synapses of other neurons on their body. However, the more frequent situation is that the body of a neuron has synapses with axons of many other neurons. It even appears that, occasionally, several axons from one neuron form synapses on another. Thus the possible stimulators are many, and the patterns of stimulation that may be effective have more complicated definitions than the simple "and" and "or" schemes described above. If there are many synapses on a single nerve cell, the simplest rule of behavior for the latter will be to respond only when it receives a certain minimum number of (simultaneous) nerve pulses (or more). However, there is some plausibility in assuming that things can, in reality, be even more complicated than this. It may well be that certain nerve pulse combinations will stimulate a given neuron not simply by virtue of their number but also by virtue of the spatial relations of the synapses to which they arrive. That is, one may have to face situations in which there are, say, hundreds of synapses on a single nerve cell, and the combinations of stimulations on these that are effective (that generate a response pulse in the last-mentioned neuron) are characterized not only by their number but also by their coverage of certain special regions on that neuron (on its body or on its dendrite system, cf. above), by the spatial relations of such regions to each other, and by even more complicated quantitative and geometrical relationships that might be relevant.

The Threshold

If the criterion of effectiveness of stimulation is the simplest one mentioned above: the (simultaneous) presence of a minimum number of stimulating pulses, this minimum-required stimulation is called the threshold of the neuron in question. It is customary to talk of the stimulation requirements of a given neuron in terms of this criterion, i.e. of its threshold. It must be remembered, however, that it is by no means established that the stimulation requirement has this simple character—it may turn around much more complicated relationships than the mere attainment of a threshold (i.e. of a minimum number of simultaneous stimulations), as discussed above.

The Summation Time

Apart from these, the properties of a neuron may exhibit other complexities which are not described by the mere stimulus-response relationship in terms of standard nerve pulses.

Thus wherever "simultaneity" is mentioned in the above, it cannot and does not mean actual, exact simultaneity. In each case there is a finite period of grace, a *summation time*, such that two pulses arriving within such a time period still act as if they had been simultaneous. Actually, things may be even more complicated than this—the summation time may not be a sharp concept. Even after a slightly longer time, the previous pulse may still be summed to the subsequent one, to a gradually decreasing, partial extent; sequences of pulses, further apart (within limits) than the summation time might, by virtue of their length, have more than the individual effect; various superpositions of the phenomena of fatigue and recovery may put a neuron into abnormal states, i.e. such where its response characteristics are different from what they are in the standard condition. On all these matters certain (more or less incomplete) bodies of observation exist, and they all indicate that the individual neuron may be—at least in suitable special situations—a much more complicated mechanism than the dogmatic description in terms of stimulus-response, following the simple pattern of elementary logical operations, can express.

Stimulation Criteria for Receptors

Only a few things need be said (in the particular, present context) about the stimulation of neurons by factors other than the outputs (nerve pulses) of other neurons. As discussed earlier, such factors are phenomena in the outside world (i.e. on the surface of the organism) to which the neuron in question is specifically sensitive (light, sound, pressure, temperature) and also physical and chemical changes within the organism at the point where the neuron is situated. Neurons whose organizational function is to respond to the first class of stimuli are commonly called *receptors*. However, it may be better to call all neurons which are organizationally meant to respond to stimuli other than nerve pulses *receptors*, and discriminate between the first and the second category by specifying them as *external* or *internal* receptors.

With respect to all of these, the question of a stimulation

criterion again arises—of a criterion defining under what conditions stimulation of a nerve pulse will take place.

The simplest stimulation criterion is again one that can be stated in terms of a threshold—just as it was in the previously considered case of the stimulation of a neuron by nerve pulses. This means that the criterion of effectiveness of stimulation can be stated in terms of a minimum intensity of the stimulating agent—i.e. a minimum intensity of illumination, of sonic energy contained in a certain frequency interval, of overpressure, of rise in temperature, respectively, for an external receptor; or a minimum change in the concentration of the critical chemical agent, or a minimum change in the value of the relevant physical parameter, in the case of an internal receptor.

It should be noted, however, that the threshold-type stimulation criterion is not the only possible one. Thus in the optical case, it appears that many of the neurons involved respond to a change of illumination (in some cases from light to dark, in others from dark to light), rather than to the attainment of a specific level of illumination. It could be that these are reactions not of a single neuron but of the neuronic output of more complicated neuron systems. I will not go into this question here. It suffices to observe that the available evidence tends to indicate that in the case of receptors, too, the threshold-type stimulation criterion is not the only one used in the nervous system.

Let me, then, repeat the above-mentioned, typical example. It is well known that in the optic nerve certain fibers respond not to any particular (minimum) level of illumination but only to changes of this level, e.g. in certain fibers it is the passage from darkness to light, in others, the passage from light to darkness which causes responses. In other words, it is increases or decreases of the level in question, i.e. the size of its derivative and not its own size, which furnish the stimulation criterion.

It would appear to be proper now to say a few things about the role of these "complexities" of the nervous system in its functional structure and its functioning. For one thing, it is quite conceivable that these complexities play no useful functional role at all. It is, however, more interesting to point out that they might conceivably have such roles and that a few things can be said about these possibilities.

It is conceivable that in the essentially digitally-organized nervous system the complexities referred to play an analog or at least a "mixed" role. It has been suggested that by such mechanisms more recondite over-all electrical effects might influence the functioning of the nervous system. It could be that in this way certain general electrical potentials play an important role and that the system responds to the solutions of potential theoretical problems in toto, problems which are less immediate and elementary than what one normally describes by the digital criteria, stimulation criteria, etc. Since the character of the nervous system nevertheless probably is primarily digital, such effects, if real, would probably interact with digital effects, i.e. it would be a question of a "mixed system" rather than of a genuine analog one. Speculations in these directions have been indulged in by several authors; it seems quite adequate to refer with respect to them to the general literature. I will not discuss them any further, in specific terms, here.

It should be said, however, that all complications of this type mean, in terms of the counting of basic active organs as we have practiced it so far, that a nerve cell is more than a single basic active organ, and that any significant effort at counting has to recognize this. Obviously, even the more complicated stimulation criteria have this effect. If the nerve cell is activated by the stimulation of certain combinations of synapses on its body and not by others, then the significant count of basic active organs must presumably be a count of synapses rather than of nerve cells. If the situation is further refined by the appearance of the "mixed" phenomena referred to above, these counts get even more difficult. Already the necessity of replacing the nerve cell count by a synapsis count may increase the number of basic active organs by a considerable factor, like 10 to 100. This, and similar circumstances, ought to be borne in mind in connection with the basic active organ counts referred to so far.

Thus all the complexities referred to here may be irrelevant, but they may also endow the system with a (partial) analog character, or with a "mixed" character. In any case, they increase the count of basic active organs, if this count is to be effected by any significant criteria. This increment may well be by a factor like 10 to 100.

The Problem of Memory within the Nervous System

The discussions up to this point have not taken into account a component whose presence in the nervous system is highly plausible, if not certain—if for no other reason than that it has played a vital role in all artificial computing machines constructed to date, and its significance is, therefore, probably a matter of principle rather than of accident. I mean the memory. I will, therefore, turn now to the discussion of this component, or rather subassembly, of the nervous system.

As stated above, the presence of a memory—or, not improbably, of several memories—within the nervous system is a matter of surmise and postulation, but one that all experience with artificial computing automata suggests and confirms. It is just as well to admit right at the start that all physical assertions about the nature, embodiment, and location of this subassembly, or subassemblies, are equally hypothetical. We do not know where in the physically viewed nervous system a memory resides; we do not know whether it is a separate organ or a collection of specific parts of other already known organs, etc. It may well be residing in a system of specific nerves, which would then have to be a rather large system. It may well have something to do with the genetic mechanism of the body. We are as ignorant of its nature and position as were the Greeks, who suspected the location of the mind in the diaphragm. The only thing we know is that it must be a rather large-capacity memory, and that it is hard to see how a complicated automaton like the human nervous system could do without one.

Principles for Estimating the Capacity of the Memory in the Nervous System

Let me now say a few words about the probable capacity of this memory.

In artificial automata, like computing machines, there are fairly well agreed on, standard ways to assign a "capacity" to a memory, and it would appear to be reasonable to extend these to the nervous system as well. A memory can retain a certain maximum amount of information, and information can always be converted into an aggregation of binary digits, "bits." Thus a memory which can hold a thousand eight-place decimal numbers would have to be assigned a capacity of $1,000 \times 8 \times 3.32$ bits, since a decimal digit is the equivalent of approximately $\log_2 10 \sim 3.32$ bits (the reasons for this method of bookkeeping have been established in the classical works on information theory by G. E. Shannon and others). It is indeed clear that 3 decimal digits must be the equivalent of about 10 bits, since $2^{10} = 1,024$ is approximately equal to $10^3 = 1,000$. (In this way, a decimal digit corresponds approximately to $10/3 \sim 3.33$ bits.) Thus the above capacity count gives the result of 2.66×10^4 bits. By a similar argument, the information capacity represented by a letter of the printed or typewritten alphabet—one such letter being a $2 \times 26 + 35 = 88$-way alternative (the 2 representing the possibility of its being upper or lower case, the 26 the number of letters of the alphabet, and the 35 the usual number of punctuation marks, numerical symbols, and intervals, which are, of course, also relevant in this context)— has to be evaluated at $\log_2 88 \sim 6.45$. Hence, e.g., a memory which can hold a thousand such letters has a capacity of $6,450 = 6.45 \times 10^3$ bits. In the same order of ideas, memory capacities corresponding to more complicated forms of information, like geometrical shapes (of course, given with a certain specified degree of precision and resolution), color nuances (with the same qualifications as above), etc. can also be expressed in terms of standard units, i.e. bits. Memories which hold combinations of all these can then be attributed capacities resulting from the ones arrived at in conformity with the above principles, simply by addition.

Memory Capacity Estimates with These Stipulations

The memory capacity required for a modern computing machine is usually of the order of 10^5 to 10^6 bits. The memory capacities to be surmised as necessary for the functioning of the nervous system would seem to have to be a good deal larger than this, since the nervous system as such was seen above to be a considerably larger automaton than the artificial automata (e.g. computing machines) that we know. By how much the surmised memory capacity should transcend the above-quoted figure of 10^5 to 10^6 is hard to tell. However, certain rough orienting estimates can, nevertheless, be arrived at.

Thus the standard receptor would seem to accept about 14 distinct digital impressions per second, which can probably be reckoned as the same number of bits. Allowing 10^{10} nerve cells, assuming that each one of them is under suitable conditions essentially an (inner or outer) receptor, a total input of 14×10^{10} bits per second results. Assuming further, for which there is some evidence, that there is no true forgetting in the nervous system—that impressions once received may be removed from the important area of nervous activity, i.e. from the center of attention, but not truly erased—an estimate for the entirety of a normal human lifetime can be made. Putting the latter equal to, say, 60 years $\sim 2 \times 10^9$ seconds, the input over an entire lifetime, i.e. with the above stipulations, the total required memory capacity would turn out to be $14 \times 10^{10} \times 2 \times 10^9 = 2.8 \times 10^{20}$ bits. This is larger than the figure of 10^5 to 10^6, recognized as typically valid for a modern computing machine, but the excess of this number over its computing machine equivalent would not seem to be unreasonably larger than the corresponding excess that we have already observed earlier for the respective numbers of basic active organs.

Various Possible Physical Embodiments of the Memory

The question of the physical embodiment of this memory remains. For this, various authors have suggested a variety of solutions. It has been proposed to assume that the thresholds—or, more broadly stated, the stimulation criteria—for various nerve cells change with time as functions of the previous history of that cell. Thus frequent use of a nerve cell might lower its threshold, i.e. ease the requirements of its stimulation, and the like. If this were true, the memory would reside in the variability of the stimulation criteria. It is certainly a possibility, but I will not attempt to discuss it here.

A still more drastic embodiment of the same idea would be achieved by assuming that the very connections of the nerve cells, i.e. the distribution of conducting axons, vary with time. This would mean that the following state of things could exist. Conceivably, persistent disuse of an axon might make it ineffective for later use. On the other hand, very frequent (more than normal) use might give the connection that it represents a lower threshold (a facilitated stimulation criterion) over that particular path. In this case, again, certain parts of the nervous system would be variable in time and with previous history and would, thus, in and by themselves represent a memory.

Another form of memory, which is obviously present, is the genetic part of the body: the chromosomes and their constituent genes are clearly memory elements which by their state affect, and to a certain extent determine, the functioning of the entire system. Thus there is a possibility of a genetic memory system also.

There are still other forms of memory, some of which have a not inconsiderable plausibility. Thus some traits of the chemical composition of certain areas in the body might be self-perpetuating and also, therefore, possible memory elements. One should consider, then, such types of memory if one considers the genetic memory system, since the self-perpetuating properties residing in the genes can apparently also locate themselves outside the genes, in the remaining portions of the cell.

I will not go into all these possibilities and many others one could consider with equal—or, in some cases, even greater—plausibility. I would like to limit myself here to the remark that even without locating the memory in specific sets of nerve cells, a wide variety of physical embodiments of various degrees of plausibility can be—and have been—suggested for it.

Analogies with Artificial Computing Machines

Lastly, I would like to mention that systems of nerve cells, which stimulate each other in various possible cyclical ways, also constitute memories. These would be memories made up of active elements (nerve cells). In our computing machine technology such memories are in frequent and significant use; in fact, these were actually the first ones to be introduced. In vacuum-tube machines the "flip-flops," i.e. pairs of vacuum tubes that are mutually gating and controlling each other, represent this type. Transistor technology, as well as practically every other form of high-speed electronic technology, permit and indeed call for the use of flip-floplike subassemblies, and these can be used as memory elements in the same way that the flip-flops were in the early vacuum-tube computing machines.

The Underlying Componentry of the Memory Need Not Be the Same as That of the Basic Active Organs

It must be noted, however, that it is a priori unlikely that the nervous system should use such devices as the main vehicles for its memory requirements; such memories, most characteristically designated as "memories made up from basic active organs," are, in every sense that matters, extremely expensive. Modern computing machine technology started out with such arrangements—thus the first large-scale vacuum tube computing machine, the ENIAC, relied for its primary (i.e. fastest and most directly available) memory on flip-flops exclusively. However, the ENIAC had a very large size (22,000 vacuum tubes) and by present-day standards a very small, primary memory (consisting of a few dozens of ten-digit decimal numbers only). Note that the latter amounts to something like a few hundred bits—certainly less than 10^3. In present-day computing machines the proper balance between machine size and memory capacity (cf. above) is generally held to lie around something like 10^4 basic active elements, and a memory capacity of 10^5 to 10^6 bits. This is achieved by using forms of memory which are technologically entirely different from the basic active organs of the machine. Thus a vacuum tube or transistor machine might have a memory residing in an electrostatic system (a cathode ray tube), or in suitably arranged large aggregates of ferromagnetic cores, etc. I will not attempt a complete classification here, since other important forms of memory, like the acoustic delay type, the ferroelectric type, and the magnetostrictive delay type (this list could, indeed, be increased), do not fit quite so easily into such classifications. I just want to point out that the componentry used in the memory may be entirely different from the one that underlies the basic active organs.

These aspects of the matter seem to be very important for the understanding of the structure of the nervous system, and they would seem to be as yet predominantly unanswered. We know the basic active organs of the nervous system (the nerve cells). There is every reason to believe that a very large-capacity memory is associated with this system. We do most emphatically not know what type of physical entities are the basic components for the memory in question.

Digital and Analog Parts in the Nervous System

Having pointed out in the above the deep, fundamental, and wide-open problems connected with the memory aspect of the nervous system, it would seem best to go on to other questions. However, there is one more, minor aspect of the unknown memory subassembly in the nervous system, about which a few words ought to be said. These refer to the relationship between the analog and the digital (or the "mixed") parts of the nervous system. I will devote to these, in what follows, a brief and incomplete additional discussion, after which I will go on to the questions not related to the memory.

The observation I wish to make is this: processes which go through the nervous system may, as I pointed out before, change their character from digital to analog, and back to digital, etc., repeatedly. Nerve pulses, i.e. the digital part of the mechanism, may control a particular stage of such a process, e.g. the contraction of a specific muscle or the secretion of a specific chemical. This phenomenon is one belonging to the analog class, but it may be the origin of a train of nerve pulses which are due to its being sensed by suitable inner receptors. When such nerve pulses are being generated, we are back in the digital line of progression again. As mentioned above, such changes from a digital process to an analog one, and back again to a digital one, may alternate several times. Thus the nerve-pulse part of the system, which is digital, and the one involving chemical changes or mechanical dislocations due to muscular contractions, which is of the analog type, may, by alternating with each other, give any particular process a mixed character.

Role of the Genetic Mechanism in the Above Context

Now, in this context, the genetic phenomena play an especially typical role. The genes themselves are clearly parts of a digital system of components. Their effects, however, consist of stimulating the formation of specific chemicals, namely of definite enzymes that are characteristic of the gene involved, and, therefore, belong in the analog area. Thus, in this domain, a particular specific instance of the alternation between analog and digital is exhibited, i.e. this is a member of a broader class, to which I referred as such above in a more general way.

Codes and Their Role in the Control of the Functioning of a Machine

Let me now pass on to the questions involving other aspects than those of memory. By this I mean certain principles of organizing logical orders which are of considerable importance in the functioning of any complicated automaton.

First of all, let me introduce a term which is needed in the present context. A system of logical instructions that an automaton can carry out and which causes the automaton to perform some organized task is called a *code*. By logical orders, I mean things like nerve pulses appearing on the appropriate axons, in fact anything that induces a digital logical system, like the nervous system, to function in a reproducible, purposive manner.

The Concept of a Complete Code

Now, in talking about codes, the following distinction becomes immediately prominent. A code may be *complete*— i.e., to use the terminology of nerve pulses, one may have specified the sequence in which these impulses appear and the axons on which they appear. This will then, of course, define completely a specific behavior of the nervous system, or, in the above comparison, of the corresponding artificial automaton involved. In computing machines, such complete codes are sets of orders, given with all necessary specifications. If the machine is to solve a specific problem by calculation, it will have to be controlled by a complete code in this sense. The use of a modern computing machine is based on the user's ability to develop and formulate the necessary complete codes for any given problem that the machine is supposed to solve.

The Concept of a Short Code

In contrast to the complete codes, there exists another category of codes best designated as *short codes*. These are based on the following idea.

The English logician A. M. Turing showed in 1937 (and various computing machine experts have put this into practice since then in various particular ways) that it is possible to develop code instruction systems for a computing machine which cause it to behave as if it were another, specified, computing machine. Such systems of instructions which make one machine *imitate* the behavior of another are known as *short codes*. Let me go into a little more detail in the typical questions of the use and development of such short codes.

A computing machine is controlled, as I pointed out above, by codes, sequences of symbols—usually binary symbols—i.e. by strings of bits. In any set of instructions that govern the use of a particular computing machine it must be made clear which strings of bits are orders and what they are supposed to cause the machine to do.

For two different machines, these *meaningful* strings of bits need not be the same ones and, in any case, their respective effects in causing their corresponding machines to operate may well be entirely different. Thus, if a machine is provided with a set of orders that are peculiar to another machine, these will presumably be, in terms of the first machine, at least in part, *nonsense*, i.e. strings of bits which do not necessarily all belong to the family of the meaningful ones (in terms of the first-mentioned machine), or which, when "obeyed" by the first-mentioned machine, would cause it to take actions which are not part of the underlying organized plan toward the solution of a problem, the solution of which is intended, and, generally speaking, would not cause the first-mentioned machine to behave in a purposive way toward the solution of a visualized, organized task, i.e. the solution of a specific and desired problem.

The Function of a Short Code

A code, which according to Turing's schema is supposed to make one machine behave as if it were another specific machine (which is supposed to make the former imitate the latter) must do the following things. It must contain, in terms that the machine will understand (and purposively obey), instructions (further detailed parts of the code) that will cause the machine to examine every order it gets and determine whether this order has the structure appropriate to an order of the second machine. It must then contain, in terms of the order system of the first machine, sufficient orders to make the machine cause the actions to be taken that the second machine would have taken under the influence of the order in question.

The important result of Turing's is that in this way the first machine can be caused to imitate the behavior of any other machine. The order structure which it is thus caused to follow may be entirely different from that one characteristic of the first machine which is truly involved. Thus the order structure referred to may actually deal with orders of a much more complex character than those which are characteristic of the first machine: every one of these orders of the secondary machine may involve the performing of several operations by the first-mentioned machine. It may involve complicated, iterative processes, multiple actions of any kind whatsoever; generally speaking, anything that the first machine can do in any length of time and under the control of all possible order systems of any degree of complexity may now be done as if only "elementary" actions—basic, uncompounded, primitive orders—were involved.

The reason for calling such a secondary code a *short code* is, by the way, historical: these short codes were developed as an aid to coding, i.e. they resulted from the desire to be able to code more briefly for a machine than its own natural order system would allow, treating it as if it were a different machine with a more convenient, fuller order system which would allow simpler, less circumstantial and more straightforward coding.

The Logical Structure of the Nervous System

At this point, the discussion is best redirected toward another complex of questions. These are, as I pointed out previously, not connected with the problems of the memory or with the questions of complete and short codes just considered. They relate to the respective roles of logics and arithmetics in the functioning of any complicated automaton, and, specifically, of the nervous system.

Importance of the Numerical Procedures

The point involved here, one of considerable importance, is this. Any artificial automaton that has been constructed for human use, and specifically for the control of complicated processes, normally possesses a purely logical part and an arithmetical part, i.e. a part in which arithmetical processes play no role, and one in which they are of importance. This is due to the fact that it is, with our habits of thought and of expressing thought, very difficult to express any truly complicated situation without having recourse to formulae and numbers.

Thus an automaton which is to control problems of these types—constancy of temperature, or of certain pressures, or of chemical isostasy in the human body—will, if a human designer has to formulate its task, have that task defined in terms of numerical equalities or inequalities.

Interaction of Numerical Procedures with Logic

On the other hand, there may be portions of this task which can be formulated without reference to numerical relationships, i.e. in purely logical terms. Thus certain qualitative principles involving physiological response or nonresponse can be stated without recourse to numbers by merely stating qualitatively under what combinations of circumstances certain events are to take place and under what combinations they are not desired.

Reasons for Expecting High Precision Requirements

These remarks show that the nervous system, when viewed as an automaton, must definitely have an arithmetical as well as a logical part, and that the needs of arithmetics in it are just as important as those of logics. This means that we are again dealing with a computing machine in the proper sense and that a discussion in terms of the concepts familiar in computing machine theory is in order.

In view of this, the following question immediately presents itself: when looking at the nervous system as at a computing machine, with what precision is the arithmetical part to be expected to function?

This question is particularly crucial for the following reason: all experience with computing machines shows that if a computing machine has to handle as complicated arithmetical tasks as the nervous system obviously must, facilities for rather high levels of precision must be provided. The reason is that calculations are likely to be long, and in the course of long calculations not only do errors add up but also those committed early in the calculation are ampli-fied by the latter parts of it; therefore, considerably higher precision is needed than the physical nature of the problem would by itself appear to require.

Thus one would expect that the arithmetical part of the nervous system exists and, when viewed as a computing machine, must operate with considerable precision. In the familiar artificial computing machines and under the condi-tions of complexity here involved, ten- or twelve-decimal precision would not be an exaggeration.

This conclusion was well worth working out just because of, rather than in spite of, its absolute implausibility.

Nature of the System of Notations Employed: Not Digital but Statistical

As pointed out before, we know a certain amount about how the nervous system transmits numerical data. They are usu-ally transmitted by periodic or nearly periodic trains of pulses. An intensive stimulus on a receptor will cause the latter to respond each time soon after the limit of absolute refractoriness has been underpassed. A weaker stimulus will cause the receptor to respond also in a periodic or nearly periodic way, but with a somewhat lower frequency, since now not only the limit of absolute refractoriness but even a limit of a certain relative refractoriness will have to be under-passed before each next response becomes possible. Consequently, intensities of quantitative stimuli are rendered by periodic or nearly periodic pulse trains, the frequency always being a monotone function of the intensity of the stimulus. This is a sort of frequency-modulated system of signaling; intensities are translated into frequencies. This has been directly observed in the case of certain fibers of the optic nerve and also in nerves that transmit information relative to (important) pressures.

It is noteworthy that the frequency in question is not directly equal to any intensity of stimulus, but rather that it is a monotone function of the latter. This permits the introduction of all kinds of scale effects and expressions of precision in terms that are conveniently and favorably dependent on the scales that arise.

It should be noted that the frequencies in question usually lie between 50 and 200 pulses per second.

Clearly, under the conditions, precisions like the ones mentioned above (10 to 12 decimals!) are altogether out of question. The nervous system is a computing machine which manages to do its exceedingly complicated work on a rather low level of precision: according to the above, only precision levels of 2 to 3 decimals are possible. This fact must be emphasized again and again because no known computing machine can operate reliably and significantly on such a low precision level.

Another thing should also be noted. The system described above leads not only to a low level of precision, but also to a rather high level of reliability. Indeed, clearly, if in a digital system of notations a single pulse is missing, absolute perversion of meaning, i.e. nonsense, may result. Clearly, on the other hand, if in a scheme of the above-described type a single pulse is lost, or even several pulses are lost—or unnecessarily, mistakenly, inserted—the relevant frequency, i.e. the meaning of the message, is only inessentially distorted.

Now, a question arises that has to be answered significantly: what essential inferences about the arithmetical and logical structure of the computing machine that the nervous system represents can be drawn from these apparently somewhat conflicting observations?

Arithmetical Deterioration. Roles of Arithmetical and Logical Depths

To anyone who has studied the deterioration of precision in the course of a long calculation, the answer is clear. This deterioration is due, as pointed out before, to the *accumulation* of errors by superposition, and even more by the *amplification* of errors committed early in the calculation, by the manipulations in the subsequent parts of the calculation; i.e. it is due to the considerable number of arithmetical operations that have to be performed in series, or in other words to the great *arithmetical depth* of the scheme.

The fact that there are many operations to be performed in series is, of course, just as well a characteristic of the *logical* structure of the scheme as of its arithmetical structure. It is, therefore, proper to say that all of these deterioration-of-precision phenomena are due to the great *logical depth* of the schemes one is dealing with here.

Arithmetical Precision or Logical Reliability, Alternatives

It should also be noted that the message-system used in the nervous system, as described in the above, is of an essentially *statistical* character. In other words, what matters are not the precise positions of definite markers, digits, but the statistical characteristics of their occurrence, i.e. frequencies of periodic or nearly periodic pulse-trains, etc.

Thus the nervous system appears to be using a radically different system of notation from the ones we are familiar with in ordinary arithmetics and mathematics: instead of the precise systems of markers where the position—and presence or absence—of every marker counts decisively in determining the meaning of the message, we have here a system of notations in which the meaning is conveyed by the *statistical* properties of the message. We have seen how this leads to a lower level of arithmetical precision but to a higher level of logical reliability: a deterioration in arithmetics has been traded for an improvement in logics.

Other Statistical Traits of the Message System That Could Be Used

This context now calls clearly for the asking of one more question. In the above, the frequencies of certain periodic or nearly periodic pulse-trains carried the *message*, i.e. the *information*. These were distinctly *statistical* traits of the message. Are there any other statistical properties which could similarly contribute as vehicles in the transmission of information?

So far, the only property of the message that was used to transmit information was its frequency in terms of pulses per second, it being understood that the message was a periodic or nearly periodic train of pulses.

Clearly, other traits of the (statistical) message could also be used: indeed, the frequency referred to is a property of a single train of pulses whereas every one of the relevant nerves consists of a large number of fibers, each of which transmits numerous trains of pulses. It is, therefore, perfectly plausible that certain (statistical) relationships between such trains of pulses should also transmit information. In this connection it is natural to think of various correlation-coefficients, and the like.

The Language of the Brain Not the Language of Mathematics

Pursuing this subject further gets us necessarily into questions of *language*. As pointed out, the nervous system is based on two types of communications: those which do not involve arithmetical formalisms, and those which do, i.e. communications of orders (logical ones) and communications of numbers (arithmetical ones). The former may be described as language proper, the latter as mathematics.

It is only proper to realize that language is largely a historical accident. The basic human languages are traditionally transmitted to us in various forms, but their very multiplicity proves that there is nothing absolute and necessary about them. Just as languages like Greek or Sanskrit are historical facts and not absolute logical necessities, it is only reasonable to assume that logics and mathematics are similarly historical, accidental forms of expression. They may have essential variants, i.e. they may exist in other forms than the ones to which we are accustomed. Indeed, the nature of the central nervous system and of the message systems that it transmits indicate positively that this is so. We have now accumulated sufficient evidence to see that whatever language the central nervous system is using, it is characterized by less logical and arithmetical depth than what we are normally used to. The following is an obvious example of this: the retina of the human eye performs a considerable reorganization of the visual image as perceived by the eye. Now this reorganization is effected on the retina, or to be more precise, at the point of entry of the optic nerve by means of three successive synapses only, i.e. in terms of three consecutive logical steps. The statistical character of the message system used in the arithmetics of the central nervous system and its low precision also indicate that the degeneration of precision, described earlier, cannot proceed very far in the message systems involved. Consequently, there exist here different logical structures from the ones we are ordinarily used to in logics and mathematics. They are, as pointed out before, characterized by less logical and arithmetical depth than we are used to under otherwise similar circumstances. Thus logics and mathematics in the central nervous system, when viewed as languages, must structurally be essentially different from those languages to which our common experience refers.

It also ought to be noted that the language here involved may well correspond to a short code in the sense described earlier, rather than to a complete code: when we talk mathematics, we may be discussing a *secondary* language, built on the *primary* language truly used by the central nervous system. Thus the outward forms of our mathematics are not absolutely relevant from the point of view of evaluating what the mathematical or logical language truly used by the central nervous system is. However, the above remarks about reliability and logical and arithmetical depth prove that whatever the system is, it cannot fail to differ considerably from what we consciously and explicitly consider as mathematics.

Printed and bound by CPI Group (UK) Ltd, Croydon, CR0 4YY

10/04/2024

14481445-0001